To Barry Joyce
From Cecil

TWENTY YEARS

IN

THE WILD WEST.

TWENTY YEARS

IN

THE WILD WEST;

Or, Life in Connaught.

By MRS. HOUSTOUN,

AUTHOR OF "A YACHT VOYAGE TO TEXAS."

LONDON:

JOHN MURRAY, ALBEMARLE STREET.

1879.

LONDON :
BRADBURY, AGNEW, & CO., PRINTERS. WHITEFRIARS.

PREFACE.

In the present state of Ireland any information from a special source and gathered on the spot is likely to be useful, as enabling those at a distance to form correct conclusions respecting the country and people.

The writer of the following chapters is induced to think that the experiences of an Englishwoman living for twenty years in one of the wildest parts of the West of Ireland, isolated and apart from any society, and surrounded solely by the peasantry, may not be without value and interest.

The determination to settle on a large unreclaimed estate, amidst bogs and moors scarcely

reached by roads, was associated with a wish,
too romantic and sanguine as it turned out,
to benefit the inhabitants of a district where
resident landlords are scarce.   How these in-
tentions were frustrated by the calamities of
Spiritual tyranny and a Reign of terror, is
explained in the following pages, a perusal of
which may possibly also be found to throw
light on the relations between LANDLORD and
TENANT, PRIEST and PEOPLE.

It is possible that in the following pages I
have not been sufficiently explicit regarding
the hostility of the Priests to ourselves.   It is
proper, therefore, to state here as an explanation of our position as English settlers in
Ireland, that almost immediately after our
arrival, the denunciation from the altar began.
In proof of this I need only refer to the local
newspapers, to Reports made to Government

by the Police who attended "Chapel," and who listened to the encouragements to the people "to take the law into their own hands," and to the consequent establishment of additional stations of constabulary in our neighbourhood in order to protect us.

CONTENTS.

CHAPTER I.

TWENTY YEARS IN THE WILD WEST.

CHAPTER I.

DEPARTURE FOR THE WEST.—IGNORANCE OF THE COUNTRY.—
THE IRISH CHANNEL *GRIEVANCE*.—ARRIVAL AT WESTPORT.

WITHIN the memory—not only of the old, but of the middle-aged—is an especially dark page in the history of our country; a page in which the great and overwhelming sufferings of a people, at no time especially favoured by the blessings of prosperity, were written in such soul-harrowing words that the heart of the British nation was aroused, as that of one man, to pity and to succour.

It was from the far, far West of the Irish Isle that the loudest cry arose,—the cry that there was famine throughout the land! Not from "lack of moisture." The gracious rain, which, as we are told, descends alike " upon the just and upon the unjust," had fallen—with perhaps even more than its usual lavish prodigality—upon the rocks and bogs of the West of Ireland, and as the clouds which perpetually hover over the Province of Connaught, do not as a rule " drop fatness," it came to pass that the crop, which formed the staple article of food for the poor inhabitants of the country, suddenly and completely failed them, and, in consequence, the famine was " sore in the land."

Of this famine (notwithstanding the generous help afforded by England) untold numbers perished. Many died from actual starvation, but far greater numbers still succumbed to fever of a low and putrid type : " *the* faver," in short, as it is familiarly called in the poverty-stricken land, where dirt, bad and inadequate food, and generally neglected drainage, are in themselves causes amply sufficient to account for the prevalence of this fell and quickly spreading disease.

During the worst years of the misery of which I speak, to obtain the rents due on the wretched " holdings " inhabited by the " finest pisantry " (oh, ghastly irony !) " on God's airth," was simply impossible ; and in consequence of this impossibility, such

amongst the many extensive landowners in the far
West as possessed no source of income save what
was drawn from the rents (usually exorbitantly
high) levied on their luckless tenantry, were *forced*,
by the actual pressure of their own wants, to become
for the time being, *non* " absentees."

In the mountainous district of wild, uncivilised
Connaught (which is divided from Connemara in
County Galway by the glorious bay—or rather arm
of the sea—known as " The Killaries"), depopulation,
owing chiefly to the causes which I have already
mentioned, had been very swiftly as well as sum-
marily carried out. With the exception of "occasional" patches, "cultivation" of the land, that in
"good" times went very far towards swelling the
rent-roll of absentee landlords, was to the luckless
tenant an extremely unremunerative process. Excepting for grazing purposes—the " stock " being, in
that case, of the hardiest description—the mountain
and moorlands (sandstone rock and hopeless tracks
of bog being agreeable varieties in this monotony of
sterility) were practically valueless. And yet these
misguided tenants, endowed—cursed, I should rather
say—with a passionate fondness for land, exceeding
even that of the Irish in other districts, clung to

their barren acres with a love that proved, in numberless instances, far stronger than the fear of death.
In their unroofed homes they would die ; and there,
amongst their own people, would they be buried.

To weary and pain my readers by dwelling alike
upon the sufferings of the poor, and the mistakes—
many and unrectifiable—of the well-meaning who
gave money, time, and counsel to those who so
sorely needed all the aid that human hearts and
heads could bestow—is far from my intention. With
those excellent ones—with the few (comparatively
speaking) who "gave of their abundance," and
with the many "middle" and "lower" class sympathisers, who, lacking "abundance," did, like the
widow in Holy Writ, "what *they* could," we have no
claim whatever to be classed. Neither my fellow
emigrant nor I had hitherto even so much as set
our feet on Irish shores—shores which had looked so
green and lovely, when only a very few short sum-
mers before, on our return from a voyage across the
Atlantic, we had gazed with rejoicing eyes at Kerry's
verdure-clothed mountains. In common with the
majority of Saxons who have never sojourned in the
"sister" island, our prejudices ran rather in favour
of its inhabitants. Those amongst them, with whom

we had come in contact in America, were perhaps
favourable specimens of their race. As sailors, too,
they were cheerful, willing, and occasionally *funny*,
whilst—as though to make amends for a dislike to
soap and water which nothing appeared able to
overcome—it must to their credit be recorded that
neither 'Philleen,' 'Kelly,' nor 'Tim' were ever
known to "sulk."

And the same may be said of the rosy-cheeked,
blue-eyed Kates and Biddys, who acted as chamber-
maids in the monster hotels, and who, in more senses
than one, were so infinitely more agreeable than the
"coloured" attendants—the "yellow gals" and boys,
who, but for the frequently arriving importations
from the Emerald Isle, would have monopolised the
well-paid appointments which they helped to fill.
As a rule, it is the better classes—both morally and
physically—of the Irish peasantry who seek a new
home in the far-away land, where the brogue is as
unwelcome as it is familiar to the ear; to us, however, who were (with the reckless courage which,
being the outcome of ignorance, deserves but little
praise) about to adventure ourselves amongst an
almost unknown people, the truth that it was (so to
speak) the dregs of the peasantry who remained at

home, was one which we had yet, and to our cost, to learn. The bitter and unquenchable hatred of the Celt towards the Saxon was, equally to us, an unknown evil. Only by slow degrees did the reality of this detestation come home to us, and sorely had we to rue a condition of things which no efforts on our part could overcome or even alleviate.

To enter into any of the circumstances, by which we were led to take a step that caused amongst our acquaintances no little surprise, would be worse than needless ; suffice it to say, that after a due portion of time and money had been expended in preliminary correspondence, and in the drawing up and signing of law papers, &c., &c., I, the weaker power in the state, was informed that everything was in readiness for " occupation," that the ruling one was lease-holder, at a low rent and for what *then* seemed an interminable number of years, of a tract of bog, lake, mountain, rock, and river, to the extent of somewhat under ninety square miles, and that it behoved me at once to commence my preparations for departure.

In the darkest ignorance of what lay before me were those preparations made. That a tent had to be pitched, or rather (to descend to matters of fact),

that a house had to be built in the heart of the
"wilds" for our accommodation, was a fact of which
I had been duly informed, but of the nature of the
"wilds" in which that highly necessary outcome of
civilisation was to be erected, my ignorance was
of the darkest. Fearing nothing, and believing
(according to my wont) *everything* which, in favour
of the last "new scheme," was brought forward in
the way of panegyric, I did not trouble myself to
make enquiries regarding that which, in point of fact,
partook not a little of the nature of the inevitable.

It was on a gloomy day in November that we commenced our pilgrimage, the termination of which
was the temporary home in which we were destined
to abide till such time as the difficult process of
erecting a suitable residence in the heart of the
Mayo Mountains should have been satisfactorily
carried out.

My first experience of the amenities of the Irish
Channel was anything but encouraging, for in the
days I write of there were no big steamers, such as
those now on the station. The vessels that plied,
carrying mails and passengers across the Irish Sea,
were little larger than those which between France
and England have been a million times anathema-

tised by the sea-sick victims who crowd their decks
and cabins; whilst, on an average, considerably
more than three times as long was required by
the Irish boats as by the Dover and Calais ones
to effect the transit. On the wretchedness which,
during a passage of seven hours, was endured in
those tossing, pitching little steamers, it is needless
to dwell. "Justice," as regards an improvement in
this matter, has at last been "done to Ireland;"
but whilst the evil (one which did, in fact, continue
during ten years of our sojourn in the land) remained in *statu quo*, it was difficult not to cordially
endorse the opinion enunciated many a long year
ago by one who knew the sister country and its *soi-
disant* grievances well, that to search farther afield
than the existence of the Irish Channel for causes
why *true* union between the two countries is morally
as well as physically impossible may be called a
decided work of supererogation.

But enough, and more than enough, of lingerings
by the way, and of speculations concerning a subject
which has for centuries defied the united wisdom of
statesmen and philosophers, and the shrewd guesses
of friends as well as foes to throw what may fairly
be called a satisfactory light upon its intricacies.

The short autumnal twilight had closed in before
we arrived in the immediate neighbourhood of the
beautifully situated town of Westport. We had
journeyed in a kind of nondescript hired vehicle,
which was slowly drawn through the muddy roads,
and up and down many a hill, by a pair of lean, ill-
fed horses, and through the roof of which the persevering rain-drops trickled. A high stone wall, prison-
like in its elevation and solidity, became suddenly
visible through the gathering misty darkness, and as
the postboy, in preparation for a more than usually
steep descent, at that moment left his tired steeds
in order to lock the wheel, I put my head out of the
only window that was capable of being opened from
the interior of the carriage, and enquired, in the
plainest English I could muster, whom the wall
belonged to.

"Shure thin, ma-am," responded the man, the tones
of his voice clearly denoting surprise at my ignorance,
"it's the Cassle itself as the wall belongs to, an' a grate
one it is enthirely, the gratest, praised be to God, in
the three counties," and having thus, evidently to his
own satisfaction, done his best to set down a benighted Saxon, the man mounted his jaded beast
once more, and with a loud cracking of whip, and

sundry indistinct accompaniments of oaths and indis-
criminate remonstrances, rattled down the steep in-
cline, over a river spanned by a gothic arch, and
past a sharp turning—the perils of which the rapidly
increasing darkness mercifully hid from our sight—
into the Town.

CHAPTER II.

BEING both weary and chilled—for four mortal
hours had been expended in the task of drawing our
carriage a distance of fifteen English miles—there
was something decidedly cheering in the sight
which met our eyes on our arrival at the door of the
only "decent" hotel of which the town of Westport
could boast. Two waiters—one, a young man with
a bald head, and the other, a very old retainer, from
whose "fell of grizzled hair" at least two ordinary
wigs might have been manufactured—flourished
flaming tallow candles in our faces, whilst in the
background, her rosy, handsome face illuminated,
not only by more tallow candles, but by smiles of
cordial welcome, stood the landlady, ready—and
that almost literally—with open arms, to receive us.

"Ye'r welcome," was her salutation when we
found ourselves within speaking distance of this

most popular of hotel proprietresses. "And shure," she added, kindly, "ye most be desthroyed entirely with the weather. Rin, Biddy, and see, is there a good fire in the parlour above stairs."

"A thousand thanks," I replied, "but as we intend to stay only for a few minutes to warm ourselves, had we not better remain by *this* fire?" making my way, as I spoke, towards a huge stack of brightly burning turf that was visible through an open door on the left, and the very sight of which disinclined us to trust to doubtful blessings in the grate above.

"Ach now, but I wouldn't be letting yer be in the public room," began our oppressively polite landlady, with beaming smiles that displayed the most perfect of teeth; but before she could proceed with her expostulation, we were already in the contemned apartment, enjoying the welcome heat which the well-dried turf threw out.

Mrs. Daly, on hospitable thoughts intent, hovered about us.

"And will ye take nothing the night? A cup o' tay, while the horses are having a sup o' male?"

"No, thank you. We had some at Oughterade, and we are in a hurry to get on to Ross;" the landlady, at this announcement, turned up her handsome nose, and truly, if she, in her own portly person, had had experience of what "tea at Oughterade" is, she could hardly—as an expression of dispraise—have elevated her nasal organ too highly.

"Ach thin, I'm thinking," and an air of serious reflection suddenly took the place of a banished smile, "that it's spring-tide, and maybe ye'll be kept by the say at the turn of the road, from gitting along. Patheen," to a man in a glazed hat who was hanging, with a number of others, apparently idle loafers, about the passage, "whin will it be the top of the tide, the night? In an hour's time, I'm thinking?"

But before "Patheen"—who was scratching his head in search of inspirations wherewith to discover what might be "the mistress'" wishes—could reply, a stout, jolly-looking individual in unmistakably clerical garb, who, previously unnoticed, had been sitting in a far corner of the room with a newspaper and materials for steaming whisky punch before him, broke in with the inevitable "Ach now," as a preliminary, and at once settled the question under discussion.

Touching his somewhat shabby, rosette-adorned hat courteously, he said, addressing himself to my companion,—

"You may have to wait, *surr*, I'm thinking, near
the Newport Road for half an hour or so, if you lave
this at onst. It'ull be high-water in an hour from
this, and the spring-tides make it contrairy gitting to
Ross House, till the say falls again."

"Good Heavens! What a bore! And how long
does this inf—— does this inconvenient stoppage
last?"

"Bedad thin, in half an hour there'd be no
throuble at all at all," and I fancied that his
"riv'rence"—as the answer, in a rich County Cork
brogue rolled from his rather loosely hung lips—
cast a suspiciously knowing glance at his landlady's comely face—a face that was once more
decked in smiles, as its owner again warmly pressed
upon us the expediency of "taking something" to
keep the "cold out."

"Would ye accipt a glass o' sherry wine, now?"
was the next hospitable query. "It's from Daublin
itsel', and couldn't be better."

"I am sure of that, but perhaps a little tea——"

"Rin, Patsey, and see to the tay, and don't be
delaying now! Hurry will ye? for shure the lady's
kilt enthirely with the cauld."

"No tea for me. Hot whisky and water is

more in my line," said my fellow traveller, on whom the agreeable fumes that proceeded from the priest's tumbler, had apparently not been without their effect.

"Ye'r welcome, surr," said the cheery faced "Father," as he made room on the small table before him for the stranger's jug and glass. "And now, Biddy, my dear, like good girl, bring the matareals at onst —sugar and lemons, d'ye hear? and divle another sort of the crathur than this same,"—taking lovingly round the neck, the bottle of above proof Parliament whisky which had been provided for his own especial delectation, and winking significantly at the red-headed, capless, serving-maid who, with her broad mouth extended with a sympathetic grin, hastened to do her pastor's bidding.

But notwithstanding the excellence of the potheen, and the conversation of Father O'Rourke (I should rather say of "The Dane"—by which title we heard the jolly-looking *habitué* of the "Royal Hotel" ad-dressed) our stay in Mrs. Daly's public room was of short duration. Brief, however, though it was, our hostess, who had quietly seated herself near the tea table, (thus compelling me, through a weak fear of hurting her *amour propre*, to swallow a

whole cupful of the wondrous decoction to which
she applied the name of "tay") found time to
make me acquainted with many facts that were
of personal interest to herself, and also possibly to
the town, amongst the most important inhabitants
of which, I doubted not, she ranked.

As the mother of twenty living children, this
buxom, comely creature, who "looked" no older
than thirty-five, deserved, if for no other cause, a
foremost place in any civilised community; but
when to this remarkable gift of multiplication there
was added—as I in after days discovered—a large-
ness of heart and a liberality of hand of which few,
in those hard times especially, could boast, my slight
irritation at her harmless over-familiarity vanished,
and I felt only shame that I did not, as regarded
her " excellent gifts of charity," go and do likewise.

And now, darkness having completely set in, we
are once more under way. A fresh pair of horses—
one very large and bony of frame, and the other fully
two hands less in stature than its fellow—had been
unequally yoked together ; we—warmed, if not refreshed, by our brief halt, again seated ourselves on
our damp cushions, and, after a short difference of
opinion between Tom the postboy and the steeds in

question had been decided in the former's favour, with a chorus of "God speed ye's," and "Send ye safe homes," still echoing in our ears, we started on our way, if not precisely rejoicing, at least without any actual misgivings as to the future which lay, vague as "the baseless fabric of a vision," looming dark before us.

As the "Dane" had prognosticated, the "waters" had subsided by the time we reached the spot which at exceptionally high tides they cover. The narrow peninsula—three-quarters of a mile long, and in some parts not a hundred yards broad, at the extremity of which stood the very small house in which we were destined temporarily to abide—was no longer what I may perhaps be allowed to call an island; and so, after a certain amount of only necessary caution (for the sea is, in darkness, not always a welcome neighbour), we found ourselves, in the dead of the chill November night, at "home."

A lovely view—one scarcely to be surpassed in beauty by any which I have ever gazed upon—is that which may be seen, one day perhaps in sixty, from the heights, looking seaward, above the town of Westport. Travellers who have had the rare good

fortune to catch a glimpse (for, as a rule, the demons
of rain and mist are here ever busied in casting
a thick veil over bounteous Nature's charms) of the
fair prospect which Clew Bay, with its countless
islands and its grand surrounding mountains, affords,
have compared the Irish Bay to that of Naples, and
certainly, inasmuch as both are island-dotted es-
tuaries, and that high lands form the "horns" (so
to speak) of the rival bays, *some* resemblance
between the two may be admitted.   The topo-
graphical advantages are, however, entirely in favour
of the one which only needs the blessing of a genial
climate and a bright blue sky to render it perfect.
Far more numerous are the islands that are here
scattered profusely (I have heard, without believing
the assertion, that they number three hundred and
sixty-five) over her storm-tossed waters, than the
comparatively few which give life and variety to
the sunny expanse of her Italian rival.   And then
the mountains!   There are none, with the exception
of Vesuvius, which adorn the "pezzo di terra caduta
dal cielo," to compare with those which, rising to
the height of from three to four thousand feet above
the level of the sea, extend on either side of Clew
Bay, far into the broad expanse of the Atlantic,

whilst Clare Island, rising grandly in its barren loneliness, is, to all appearance, about equidistant from either of the two imposing ranges of usually cloud-capped heights—heights which (bold "giants" of this smaller " Western world ") guard with their frowning summits the entrance to the Bay. Unfortunately the description of sky which, almost perpetually, lowers above the Western coast of Ireland, is not one from which anything beautiful could, even by the most country-loving and enthusiastic of Erin's sons or daughters, be supposed to fall, and, as, on the day following that which witnessed our arrival in our almost literally sea-girt abode, Dame Nature had not the courtesy to draw aside her misty curtain in our honour, the delight of gazing on the vaunted beauties of the coast had to be postponed *sine die.*

Not that from our windows there existed, in the very brightest weather, what may be called a "prospect." Another long neck of slightly elevated and utterly barren land ran parallel with our own peninsula into the bay. When the tide was low, about fifty yards of rather unpleasantly muddy water lay between us and this barrier against what we were told was a glorious view beyond, and in the

c 2

meantime it only remained for us to make the best
of what we had, and to hope that the blessed lumi-
nary which "rules the day" would, sooner or later,
take pity upon the Saxon wanderers.

CHAPTER III.

THE first object which met my sight, as I came
down to breakfast, was a group of women, three in
number, two of them carrying each a child in her
arms, whilst sundry other little ones, miserably
clad (if clad they could be called, whose attire consisted only of rags, *how* held together seemed a
miracle to the lookers-on) and seeming, as indeed
they were, half dead with cold and hunger—whim-
pered and trembled, as they crouched beside their
mothers. On their heels, upon the rain-soaked soil
outside the kitchen door, the wretched creatures
crouched; but on catching sight of me, as I glided
by towards the breakfast room, they rose with one
accord to their feet, and such a clamour of mingled
voices arose as never before had it been my lot to
listen to.

"Arrah now, milady," screamed one poor soul, a
mother, still young in years, but on whose brow
want and misery had traced furrows deeper than
many which I have seen on the foreheads of octo-
genarians, "and won't ye, for the sake of the
childre, have pity on us the day? Sorra a bit o'
roof have the drivers left abuve us, and me a lone
widdy, wid me husband lying dead of the faver.
Och hone, och hone." And the groan with which
she closed her piteous appeal seemed to come from
the very depths of a heart on which had been laid
a burden far too heavy to be borne.

The tale—alas! a too true one—urged by another
sufferer was still more soul-harrowing. She also
was a widow. Hunger and disease had cut off, in
such poor "prime" as a Mayo "mountainy man"
ever arrives at, the Pat, or Phil, or Larry to whom—
probably at the early age of sixteen—her priest had
linked her. Ten children, all living, had been born
to them; in truth—and, to quote her own words—a
"long, wake family" was the one which, "by the
blessing of God," this poor wretch had brought into
the world to starve!

The youngest born was in her arms—a shrivelled
atom of humanity; already—to judge by the pale

violet tint which pervaded its shrunken features—
far on its way to " dusty earth."

" There's three on 'em as is nigher gone than he
be, yer honour," wailed the supplicant. " They do
be lying, the crathers—begging yer honour's pardon,
agin the stones on the mountain beyant, for sorra a
bit o' roof have the drivers left abuve their heads,
God help them, and they stritched with the faver,
and sorra a mouthful o' pratees left for 'em to ate."

It was dreadful to hear her—dreadful to look upon
her wasted features, her colourless, fleshless cheeks,
and her dying baby! For *that*, however, there was
consolation in the thought that the sinless thing I
gazed upon so pityingly was about right soon to evade
the thousand ills to which flesh is heir. " Hunger
and cold " would, in a few short hours, " trouble him
no further." From the " unrest " too, which caused
his bigger brother to well nigh wriggle himself out of
his rags, the three months' old baby would in the
grave be exempt, and I felt that little Tim, lying
white and silent on his mother's ill provided breast,
was far better out of the world in which he had
made so short a stay, than in it.

To a mother, and especially to an Irish mother,
this practical view of the case brought with it no

comfort. Wonderfully large, as I had subsequently a thousand opportunities of remarking, are the hearts of Celtic parents, as regards their numerous little ones, and, as I gazed on the wistful, loving eyes of that desolate widow, my pity for the added sorrow that was so soon to come upon her was bespoken beforehand.

The third "stranger" within our gates was to outward appearance childless. She was also a degree better clad than her companions, her figure being enveloped in one of the ample dark blue cloaks, almost habitually worn by the better-to-do amongst the Connaught peasant women, whilst her head, although, like those of my other visitors, it was now uncovered, *had* apparently during her twenty-five miles' walk, enjoyed the advantage of shelter from the rain, for the marvellous crop of hair which had once been red, but was now plentifully besprinkled with grey, was "unwashed by the shower," or rather steady small rain that was persistently falling, whilst from around her wrinkled neck there hung by its strings a much worn flannel petticoat, the which— as was easy to guess—had whilom performed the duty of protecting its owner's unkempt head from the assaults of the weather.

Drawing from beneath the folds of her cloak, a *something* which had hitherto remained concealed, the woman, holding in her skinny fingers the said something (which proved to be a living, but *very* thin goose), before my astonished gaze, looked at me askance. So utterly was I taken aback by this unexpected apparition that, for some time, I failed to understand that the long suffering animal in question had been conveyed from its owner's well-loved "holding," in the hope that I, accepting of the bird as a present—alias *bribe*—would use my influence with her landlord (with whom I had not—as may here be incidentally remarked—at that time even the pleasure of acquaintance), in her favour, and obtain from him a boon, one which is coveted by the Irish tenant with an intensity of feeling wholly unknown to Englishmen in the like position, the boon, that is, of being allowed to remain on a "bit o' land," the rent to be paid for which is generally very much out of proportion to its actual value.

I have, for two reasons, described at some length my interview with these unhappy women, my first motive for so doing being to refresh the memory of such among my readers as have either forgotten or—for what is not impossible ?—have never heard of

the Irish famine of '47 and '48, and my second
reason for so long delaying the progress of my narrative is to convey, as far as may be, some faint idea
of the misery which, without the power of lessening
it, I had come to witness, and the which, I had a
sort of " dim " cônsciousness, we had no small share
in aggravating.

During the greater portion of the ensuing winter
our doors were besieged by houseless and half-naked
wanderers from the all but depopulated mountain
district, in the centre of which our future residence
was being erected.   The impossibility of doing anything (with the exception of giving them the "bit
and sup" of which they stood so much in need) for
their relief, added immeasurably to the pain which
these visits inflicted upon me.   Utterly useless were
my attempts to reconcile anyone amongst their
numbers to even the shortest of sojourns in that
detested refuge, the "Poor House."   *Death* was to
one and all infinitely preferable to "imprisonment"
within the walls of the huge ugly building, which
raised its much-hated head on a commanding elevation outside the town of Westport.   And so it came
to pass that many did die; others who, whilst declaring their inability to pay the "rint," had laid by, in

an old stocking, good store of gold, emigrated at their own expense to America, whilst other some were sent at the landlord's expense out of the poor land they loved.   Those who remained, loathed with a deadly and unsleeping hatred (but this was a truth which had yet to be made manifest to us) the strangers and the Sassenach by whose agency alone, as they were brought to believe, they had been deprived of the blessings they had so long enjoyed, and whose flocks and herds now monopolized the dearly-prized rights of which they, the "mountainy men," were now bereft.   Truly, if all were known, our privileges were not too cheaply bought.

That the landlords, who had themselves greatly suffered during the season of destitution and misery, of which we witnessed the remaining evils, had done their utmost for the people's present relief and eventual benefit, there can be no doubt.   To permit of the continuance upon the barren mountains' sides of the wretched cotters whose very existence thereon had been productive both to themselves and to the owners of the land of nought but harm, would have been an act of scant charity to those for whose sakes great and strenuous efforts for their welfare in other lands were generously made by the landlords in the West.

CHAPTER IV.

CONTRARY to the advice, not only of our landlord,
but also of the long-headed Protestant rector of
N——, and of more than one other experienced and
unprejudiced *indigène*, the new tenant, whom I will
henceforth speak of as " the Captain " (*that* being
the appellation which, from the date of our arrival,
was universally adopted as the title of the new
settler), persisted in his previously formed determination to employ the labour of the country, and that
labour only, on the extensive grazing farm of which
he had lately become a leaseholder. Thoroughly
unsuspicious—as it is the nature of large and generous minds to be—ignorant as a child of the business
on a huge scale in which he had embarked his all,
beguiled by the specious blarney of the natives with
whom he came in contact, and last, though far from
least amongst the causes of his determination, deeply

impressed with the idea that amongst the many
evils which had tended to Ireland's lack of prosperity
the non-utilization of their "labour" and the consequently small amount of money that circulated
amongst the "lower orders" could not be counted
amongst the least—"the Captain," fearless because
ignorant of the probable consequences of his resolve,
steadily refused to listen to the advice of others more
experienced than himself.

For a time all went smoothly. We engaged an
Irish manager on the faith of his recommendations
—dubious ones, as we afterwards learned ; but no
one amongst our new acquaintances was sufficiently
interested in our well doing to run the risk—in
a country where untruthfulness is the rule, and
honest speaking the exception—of opening our eyes
to the danger of placing unbounded confidence in a
drunkard, and, as regarded his present occupation,
a wholly untried man. For a time affairs went on
smoothly. B——, with a thousand pounds or so of
his employer's money in his pockets, regularly attended
the fairs, purchasing sheep and cattle after the lavish
fashion in which the cash of other people is so often
flung about, and was supposed—an assumption which
eventually proved to have been totally unwarranted

—to spend much of his time in the mountains, which
loomed dark and lowering on the southern side of the
Bay, in the discharge of his arduous duties as steward,
superintendent, and manager. During a long and, as
is invariably the case in "the West," a very rainy
winter, the business of building proceeded but slowly
on the shores of Dhulough, or the Black Lake. Nor
could this be a matter for wonder. The rough sandstone of which the walls were built had to be
quarried from the steep mountain side. Lime could
only be procured from a long distance, a stormy sea
often endangering the safety of the "hookers," as
the country sailing boats are called, which carried
the "risky" cargo. Added to these, and a thousand
other impediments to progress, the nearest cottage
in which the workmen employed could hope to find
shelter was three miles at least from the Lough,
whilst as to a *shebeen* house, or indeed any house
where a *dhrop of crathur* comfort could be purchased there existed literally none.

B——, whose wife and large family were dwellers
in the town of Westport, was from the North of
Ireland, and consequently the trust reposed in him
as manager was unbounded. The weekly reports
which he gave to us of affairs in general, and of

the progress of "the Lodge," which in the "bleak wilderness" of Glenumra was beginning to raise its modest head aloft, were always rose-coloured, and, as such, too pleasant not to be implicitly believed. The man in fact, was boasted of by us as a perfect treasure, and our satisfaction with, and appreciation of the County Derry steward, would have been simply boundless, but for those periodical "giddinesses" of his, which, whenever they occurred, filled us with a selfish fear, for what, we asked ourselves, *should* we do without him ?

As the Spring advanced, however, it came to be— at first faintly, but by degrees more loudly—whispered that, of the several thousands of four-footed beasts by whom the "finest pisanthry in the wurrld" were said to have been replaced in "the mountains," the traces were wonderfully few and far between. Here and there, a "very odd " (to use an every-day country term) sheep, one, Irish born and bred, scraggy, scabby, woolless, might be seen alone, afflicted not uncommonly with that fell disease the staggers, and presenting to the view of the passers-by a sorry specimen of the "improved breed" which common report averred the Saxon settler was about to introduce into the country.

When questioned, which he—as a matter of necessity was—regarding the reports which had reached "the master's ears," B—— had, or he would have been no true Irishman, always an answer ready. With a lofty contempt which was really, in its way, imposing, he scouted the notion that on the wild mountain sides, and amongst the jutting rocks and dark brown heather, there were fewer animals than his employer had a right to expect. With an allowance of two acres for each sheep it was simply ridiculous, he argued, to suppose that a beast was to be met with at every turn, and as to their being "here and there a *yow* with some of her wool off, shure they would be caught sometimes in a whin-bush, the crathurs, and little the wuss of it—thanks be to God—they'd be."

This airy way of taking the matter proved for a time sufficiently reassuring. It is, as we all know, very pleasant to believe the "best," and intensely disagreeable, not only to admit that you have been wrong, but to commence the unpleasant task of undoing past work, which (by oneself at least) had been highly approved of. "Faith," too, the kind of faith which it was both comfortable and flattering to one's self love to place in the invaluable B——, had not as

yet received the very slightest shock. To the hints
which daily became stronger, that in the "mountains" all was perhaps not going on precisely as it
should do, a deaf ear was persistently turned, and
when it happened that about this time our trusted
bailiff was accidentally thrown from his dog-cart,
and rather severely cut about the head by his fall,
the way in which we nursed and petted him, providing him with luxuries, and assisting him, when
convalescent, in his work was, as the Americans say,
a "caution."

But as the Spring advanced, and the lambing
season (always, in wild *mountainy* districts, a comparatively late affair,) grew nearer and nearer, concealment as regarded the amount of "stock," in the
purchase of which so many of our precious thousands had been sunk, became no longer possible. To
make a long story short, the day of reckoning with
our rashly trusted manager came at last, and proved
an almost ruinous one to us. "Report" had not in
this case in any way exaggerated matters, for the
robbery, both as to the quantity and quality of the
"stock" purchased by B—— on our account, was
far greater than had been surmised. His practice,
as now came to light, had been to buy at the country

fairs which he attended, old, toothless, and sickly
sheep; the "quills," as they are called, of other
people's flocks; and to turn them out upon the
mountains to die. It is, perhaps, unnecessary to
add, that not only was the price nominally paid five
times in excess of that which this precious rascal
really gave for the ewes, but that the yield of lambs
was altogether short.

In justice, however, to this prince among rogues,
I deem it right to add that the temptation to cheat
was, owing to the easy goingness of his master,
almost too great to be resisted; and then it must
also be said that our ruin, for ruin *pro temp.* it was,
could not be laid at the door of his rascality alone.
As we afterwards learned, the numbers of our enemies
were as great as their cunning, and their determination to vitally injure us had been wondrous and fixed.
From headquarters, that is to say from the altars of
their priests, whose merest hint was as a sacred law
to these ignorant and bigoted people, the edict *to*
kill, *desthroy*, and "smash up" with ruthless hand
the Saxon invader of their rights had been promul-
gated immediately on its being known that we were
about to occupy the land; and well and zealously
had the benighted priest-ridden ones done their

work of destruction ! When B——, discharged
and disgraced, whiningly endeavoured, by accusing
others, to make his offences appear less monstrous
than they were, I imagine he was not far wrong in
affirming that what with sheep hurled over precipices, worried by dogs, and stolen and devoured by
the many who were in league against us, and whose
object it was to drive us with all convenient expedition from among them, the amount of "stock"
which, under the Christian auspices of the ministers
of religion, came to an untimely end, was scarcely
less than that which was lost to us through the
crafty devices of our own exemplary servant.

With this overwhelming loss, "dark night" had
set in, indeed, for us; but "Hope"—and let the
afflicted be thankful for the gift,—"Hope springs
eternal in the human breast," and the expectation of
being "blest," eventually, makes amends for many
a present seeming misfortune.

CHAPTER V.

AFTER this crushing blow, "parties" in our household were for some time divided regarding the expediency, or rather the possibility, of persevering in the scheme, as to the success of which one at least of the small conclave—*the* One, in short, who was, "by right Divine," the ruling spirit—had shown himself so sanguine. In proportion as his expectations had been (perhaps unduly) raised, his spirits were crushed now; nor were the reaction and its attendant gloom altogether to be wondered at. With a very small exception, our "all" had been swallowed up in the "venture," of which there only remained some 70,000 acres of leasehold mountains, and a few scabby sheep with which to stock them. The rent—not a heavy one, happily—had of course to be paid, and nothing short of a miracle, such as that which stocked the land of *im*patient Job a second time, seemed able to

raise us from the Slough of Despond into which we
had incontinently fallen. At this period also we
began to entertain some accurate idea of the extent
and dimensions of the dangers to which, in Ireland,
new occupiers of land, from which its former holders
have been ejected, are exposed. To do "the Captain" justice, it must be averred that the prospect
of peril, of strife, and of difficulty would, under ordinary circumstances, have been incentives rather than
otherwise to a continuance in the mode of life which
had been so inauspiciously commenced; while as regarded myself, it is questionable whether at that
time I fully or, indeed, in any degree, realised the
extent of the dangers which, in the war with priests
and natives that we had entered upon, most certainly awaited us. There was, for those belonging
to me, much to be said in favour of a state of things
which to myself personally was to the last degree
distasteful. For men, and even for boys, whose
interests—children, as they were as yet—had to be
duly considered, a Town existence in physical idleness is to the last degree objectionable. Exercise,
sport (for in the land to which we had migrated
there was no lack of God's creatures, furred, feathered,
and *finned,* to kill), together with that greatest of

blessings—*something to do,* were amongst the advantages which a residence in the priest-ridden, rain-drowned land in which we had sought a home, afforded for those who naturally objected to the misfortune of having nothing to do with their time.

The vexation of being " beaten," and the discomfort of practically confessing to having been taken in, were points of which in argument I made the most ; and finally (Ah, well a day !) I obtained the mastery of the situation. Negotiations for loans— (Alas ! we could no longer trade on that which was our own)—were commenced. A sum of money sufficient for very limited stocking of the land was raised on the security of the lease ; and one good generous fellow lent, after the fashion of his kind, every pound he possessed, without any security at all !

And so, under grievously altered circumstances, we recommenced work afresh. A new manager took our affairs in hand, a better system of supervision was organised, and we began once more, with tolerable composure, to look our future in the face.

Amongst the events which occurred during the ensuing summer, I must not omit to mention one

which at the time considerably interested not only
us, but the County Mayo at large. This event was
one of no less importance than an election for the
County, and as "parties," Protestants and Roman
Catholics, ran tremendously high in the country, the
occasion was likely to prove, to say the least of it,
exciting.   The Protestant candidate was an ex-
Colonel of Cavalry, possessed of no inconsiderable
extent of land in the neighbourhood of the County
Town, but who was, though an Irishman, dull of wit ;
whilst his opponent, the nominee of the priests, joined
to the advantages of being a bigoted Papist those of
having made a name, whether for good or evil, on
the Turf, and of being, " which nobody could deny,"
" a jolly good fellow," and one who always had his
wits about him.

When I look back, through the long vista of past
years, upon the intensity of interest which I took in
the result of that violently contested election, a great
wonder that so it should have been takes possession
of my mind.   The Colonel was an old acquaintance,
and a kind and hospitable man, but as to his presence
in the House of Commons being likely to conduce
in the slightest degree to the good of any living
being, *that,* no one acquainted with the quondam

Light Cavalry officer could expect. To the priest's
candidate I entertained no personal objection, but I
do confess to having indulged in eager longings that
those evil-looking, black visaged men—(for during
all the years I passed in Ireland, I never remember
to have seen a fair complexioned priest)—who, to
the discredit of their sacred profession, lawlessly in-
terfered in political agitation—thereby spreading disaffection and encouraging drunkenness and violence
—might be put down, on this occasion at least, by a
signal defeat.

To this end I, in a quiet way, was rash enough to
work, striving to the best of my powers, but alas!
entirely in vain, to snatch, if such a thing were
possible, one vote at least from the grasping hands
of the R. C. party. As may be supposed, my proceedings very soon became publicly known, nor was
it long before I received a rather significant warning
to desist from the work I had undertaken. This
warning was no other than the throwing of a big
stone—Pat is a first-rate hand at hurling—in the
direction of, or rather *at* my head, as I rode at a
foot's pace past a field in which some labourers,
women as well as men, were digging potatoes. The
missile must have been brought there ready to hand,

for, as a rule, stones are not to be found in long established potato grounds, and my almost daily habit of riding into the town of Westport to help make music for a sweet and patient lady who lay dying within " the Cassle" walls, had come to be well known.

I felt, as the saying is, the " wind " of the projectile as it whizzed within an inch of my ear; and, but for that inch, I should probably have been a dead woman. " A miss is," as we all know, " as good as a mile," and as I cantered off, waving my hand in *grateful* acknowledgment to the group, a laugh that had in its tone but little of merriment followed me on my forward way.

And now, the day appointed for the nomination has come at last, and we are on our way—fully armed and accoutred—to the scene of the election, namely, the county town, from which we are distant some dozen miles or so of a cross country but nevertheless well kept road, along which, seeing that we met but few human beings on the way, our progress was satisfactory enough. The duty of driving devolved on me, for " the Captain " had, less than a week before, been thrown from his dog-cart and had dislocated his left shoulder. Our carriage was a low phaeton ; between us there reposed a loaded pistol, whilst the back seat contained the coachman and stable helper, each armed with a pistol.

Gaily our handsome pair of "well-bred ones" trotted along the hilly road, past ruined and roofless cottages—sad monuments of the many evils which selfishness, misrule, a scheming priesthood, and "the act of God" (that is, the famine) had brought upon the people—and also past more than one specimen of the hideous description of architecture peculiar to the ancient Irish castle in which Brian Boru and other Celtic notabilities are supposed to have lived and flourished. Until we arrived within a mile or so of Castlebar, only one incident, and that a brief one, had occurred to remind us of the fact that on that lovely June day we were journeying through a hostile country, one, in short, in which the worst passions of human nature had been unchained by those who ought to have kept them in check.

As we passed a sharp turn in the road, which had been concealed, as had also been some cabins, by intervening trees, half-a-dozen women, or rather I should call them furies—so wild did they look, and so violent were their gestures—dashed out of the cabins to meet us, and if possible to stay our progress. In the hand of each was that formidable weapon—a stocking with a stone in it—and well-prepared were these furies in female form to use upon us the arms with which they had provided themselves. Happily, however, for all concerned, their devices were frustrated, for the horses after a tremendous start and swerve which nearly lodged one "enemy" in the ditch, and sent the others flying helter-skelter away, darted off at full speed along the road, bearing us off unscathed.

It was by a back street leading to the market place and Town Hall, that we made our entrance into the town, and were met by a tolerably large, and not a little tipsy, detachment of the foe. With a savage yell they greeted us, and there was an instantaneous rush, not only at the horses' heads, but at our own persons by sundry of the most daring of the crew. One man—I can see him before me now—a gaunt, hungry-looking fellow, with a thoroughly Irish, that is to say *animal* mouth, and long hair, matted and dirty, covering his hatless head, had the temerity to lay his grimy fingers on my spotless reins ; but in the twinkling of an eye "the Captain's" pistol was at his head, the cold steel touching his temple, while a voice of thunder cried, "You d—d scoundrel, if you don't leave hold this moment, you're a dead man;" and so in very truth, had he not obeyed the order, the deluded Celt, who, plied with whisky by his priest, was only doing what he deemed his duty, would have been; but fortunately the instinct of self-preservation was strong within him, and, letting go the reins, he fell back amongst the crowd. The mere sight of the pistol worked wonders on the frightened throng. To be sure, as each man probably argued, if fired it could only kill one amongst their number, but then who could be certain that that one would not be the precious *ego* whose fears led him to take, with the least possible delay, refuge behind his comrade's back, a movement which being tolerably general, enabled me, by dashing suddenly forward, to "scatter mine enemies and make them flee." In another twenty seconds some heavy dragoons, a squadron of whose regiment had been sent from a distance to "keep the peace," closed round us, and we were escorted in safety to the Court-house.

With the exception of a brigade of scowling priests who, here and there and everywhere appeared the presiding genii—(I wish I could say, the

good genii)—of the place, there was nothing in the
business of nomination that was worthy of especial
record. The racing candidate.was caustic, amusing,
and, *tant soit peu*, coarse in both his ridicule and
abuse of his opponent ; whilst the latter, open-
mouthed and open-eyed in his surprise that a man
whom he had considered to be his friend, and to
whom his house had been always hospitably open,
could display so vast an amount of ingratitude, had
scarcely a word to say for himself.

With the help of the soldiers, and also owing to
the shelter of a big cotton umbrella, with which the
coachman warded off. several showers of stones, we
escaped without injury from the scene of action ; but
remembering that to the frequent exhortations to
violence that proceeded from the altars of the Romish
chapels might be traced that letting loose of evil
passions, and that virulent hatred of class and creed,
which made men for the time as murderers, no thinking mind could fail to be stirred, and that to the
very depths, by the sights and sounds we had been
witnessing.

I may here say, *en passant*, that in the teeth of
opposition stronger and more persistent on the part
of the Protestant landlords than had been known for

many a day—and although every precaution had
been taken to prevent violence and coercion—by
placing in safe custody and under lock and key,
voters who ran risks of being tampered with by the
other side, the priests—as had generally been foreseen
—came victors out of a contest which, but for certain
peculiarities of the " times " in which it occurred,
would not have been allowed to occupy in its
description so many pages in my narrative.

I have been desirous to show that the " famine,"
whilst it took, as the saying went, " the heart out
of the people," was far from producing a similar
effect upon those who (in the far West, at least),
I do not greatly err in calling their Rulers. The
rapid diminution of the population, from the very
existence of which the revenues of the priesthood
are derived, seemed to have produced no other
effect than that of stimulating to fresh exertions
the men whose pockets the evils attendant on
the famine had, for the time being, stripped of
their accustomed resources. The lack of spirit and
courage in their flocks was in favour rather than
otherwise of their pastor's success ; for it was on
the fears and superstition of a timorous people that
" the clergy " chiefly traded ; whilst, as regarded the

return to Parliament of a papist whom they could *trust*, it may be fairly asserted, that as long as whisky was attainable, (especially when strengthened by the adulteration of vitriol, and other deleterious drugs), the Pope's henchmen in the West had things pretty much their own way.

From the early days of Jewish history, when the priests of Baal contended against the anointed ones of the Lord, religious animosity, even when *not* stirred and fomented by greed of gain, has— as all the world will admit—been amongst the most fruitful causes of human strife and hatred; and, this being so, some excuse for the especially truculent condition of mind by which, at the period in question, the Romish clergy rendered themselves remarkable, may be found in the much talked about proselytising "Mission to Achill." Into the very heart of the enemy's country had the zealous, but injudicious, "Bible Christians" marched, and taking advantage of the bitter distress which reigned supreme in the heart of Achill's barren mountains, they, acting, I suppose, on the old principle, that, in love (*Christian* to wit) and war, all stratagems are fair, commenced their operations with a fervour and zeal which too often outran discretion. Loud

and jubilant was the cry which from Exeter Hall
echoed through Protestant England, when the first
results of the Achill Mission were proclaimed in
glowing terms.   Nor were the sinews of war wanting.   Subscriptions for the building of Protestant
schools, and even of Protestant churches, flowed in
apace.   Converts to the new faith were—well, not
allowed to starve, whilst " their riv'rences, the clergy,"
though supine in appearance and manners, kept
their eyes wide open, and

" Piled on human heads the mountain of their curses."

Taught by them to " lie with silence," the pseudo
converts, while not by one single hair's breadth
shaken from the " Faith that was their fathers',"
attended (their priest permitting) the services of the
Reformed Church, and were added to the list of
those who, " plucked like a brand from the burning,"
owed their salvation to the large Charity of Exeter
Hall sympathisers in their cause.   As to any real
or permanent conversion of the Irish peasants to
Protestantism, the " Mission " was wholly unsuc-
cessful.

CHAPTER VI.

EVILS OF ABSENTEEISM.—EXCUSES TO BE FOUND IN THE
CLIMATE OF THE WEST OF IRELAND.—LOSS OF THE OLD
FEUDAL FEELING.

If the Reader, as is highly probable, has never
chanced to visit the seaport town of Westport, he
will find it difficult to realise, from description, either
the beauty of its site, or the squalid ugliness of
its streets and buildings. The "God" who "made
the country" did, as ever, His work right well; but
the hand of "man who makes the town," has terribly
marred the loveliness of Nature's face, a truth which
is especially evident on a near inspection.

The valley, in which this unseemly collection of
ugly and dilapidated buildings lies snugly en-
sconced, is situated at the head of Clew Bay, and
enjoys the privilege of having in its midst a rapid
and brawling river, which, after running through the
town, finds its way, in winding beauty, through
the Marquis of Sligo's Park into the sea. On

E

all sides, save one, the heights are well wooded,
and the white walls of the Convent of our Lady of
Mercy, of which a view is caught from amongst the
surrounding trees, produces a really charming effect;
an effect, however, which on a closer view of the
place is worse than lost, so dreary, so decaying, and
so desolate are the sights which everywhere meet
the eye. On the principle that "beauty," as regards the exterior of buildings (and indeed not in
that matter alone) is very much an affair of money,
it is but charitable to conclude that lack of funds is
as much answerable, as is deficiency of taste, for the
universal ugliness which, both in town and country
—in the dwellings of the so-called "great," as well
as in those of the middle and lower classes—is, in
Ireland, so remarkable a feature. Square of form,
flat of face, with small windows put in solely for
use, ornament of any kind being almost invariably
wanting, such are among the outward characteristics
of the generality of Hibernian houses; and when, as
is (or, it would be perhaps more discreet to say *was*)
the case with the town I am describing, very many
of the said flat-faced, slate-roofed dwellings were
fast falling to ruin, their doors hanging loosely on
the hinges, and the broken panes of the windows

stuffed with dirty rags, far stronger and more painful
feelings than that which the absence of what we are
accustomed to call "taste" is apt to call forth, are
awakened in the spectator's mind. For what, he
can hardly fail to ask himself, is the *primary* cause
of the desolation, which, in animate as well as
inanimate things, he sees around him ? Not—I
boldly affirm—the Famine. The decay, and apparently hopeless retrogression of a town which
must have once possessed a future, a town advanta-
geously situated as regards facilities for mercantile
ventures, and which enjoys (?) the privilege of
standing on soil belonging to a landlord whose
nominal rent roll was many thousands per annum,
and the gates leading to whose park and mansion
may almost literally be said to form an adjunct of
the town, must be traced to causes anterior to the
heavy calamities with which the land had of late
been visited; and the chief of those causes (I had
been about to say, the only one) is that curse of the
country, *Absenteeism.* In the County Mayo, one of
the most extensive in Ireland, the proportion of
landowners who, from selfishness and lack of
patriotism, live away from, and spend their income
out of, the country, is very large. "Is it absentees

E 2

you mane?" an Irishman is known once to have
said, "Shure we've *lashings of 'em* * between this
and Dublin;" and, laugh as we may at the blunder,
who that has ever witnessed the results of the fact
can think of it without reprobation and regret?
During the long years which I, an English woman,
and a stranger, wearily passed in a land which so many
wealthy Irishmen avoid as they would one plague-
stricken, I can safely enunciate my belief, that, in
the no inconsiderable portion of it which came
under my notice, very few landlords *practically*
evinced the slightest inclination to sojourn on their
estates.   Those of the numbers who cared for
"sport" might, during the shooting season, spend a
few weeks on the mountains or in the woods; and
"business," that is, the overhauling an agent's accounts, and such like important matters, did, at
certain seasons of the year, draw from their more
agreeable homes elsewhere the owners of the soil;
but,—and alas! for the neglected people, for whose
well-being they were, and are, to a large extent,
answerable,—no sense of duty, and no willingness of
self-sacrifice, prompted that expenditure *in* the

---

* *Anglicè,* "lots of them."

country of the money that they derived from it,
which alone could effectually benefit that country,
and be a lasting credit to themselves.

Most willing am I to own that of all localities
under—I was about to say, the sun!—the West of
Ireland is the very last in which I, for one, would
choose to pitch my tent. "The rain it raineth
every day," and for the sight and warmth of the
glorious sun you pine in vain. The commonest
fruits—such as cherries, pears, and plums, rarely
ripen out-of-doors, while—flavourless in comparison
with those of more sunny lands—even the lower
products of the kitchen garden bear witness to
the ungenial nature of the climate in which they
live. I do not hesitate to assert that, during my
twenty years of residence, the occasions on which I
recognised the flavour of an English raspberry or
strawberry were rare enough to be individually
remembered. And then—how totally deficient in
most of the sights and sounds which render Summer
and Autumn in rural England charming, is the "land
of shade and storms" in which our lot was cast.
The pleasant prospect of crops ripening for the sickle,
of sunny harvest gatherings, and of hayfields whence
comes floating over the smiling meadows the aroma

of the drying grass, than which no scent is sweeter, these are amongst the simple but accustomed pleasures, which in the wet Province of Connaught, can rarely be enjoyed; for in nine seasons out of ten the sheaves of oats and barley stand—melancholy monuments of useless industry—on the rain-soaked bogland till the grain "grows" in the ear, and the crop is useless save for forage. Nor does the hay-making time present, as a rule, more encouraging prospects, for generally speaking the "saving" process, as it is called, is not effected, till (owing to often repeated "spreadings," and long continued existence in the shape of most forlorn looking "cocks,") the whole is too mouldy to be serviceable. Potato fields, however useful, are not, as we all must admit, picturesque, and the same may be said of that very considerable extent of Irish acreage, from which the bog-diggers obtain the fuel of the country, and cut the "turrf" ruthlessly away from both roadside and pasture.

But if it be the fact that climate has much to do with rendering the West of Ireland unpopular, may not something also as regards the character and proceedings of the *indigènes* be urged in excuse of those who, throwing Duty and Principle to the winds,

decline to cast in their lot amongst them ? To this
I answer that the western Irish are *now* very much
what the lords of the soil have made them. Time
was, and that not so very long ago, when in no
people on earth was the feeling of feudal attachment
so strong and so devoted as in the hearts which
absenteeism, lack of sympathy, and hard exaction of
rentals to be paid, have now so effectually alienated.
At the time when we made our *entrée* on the scene,
the hereditary respect and devotion of the tenantry
to the " ould family," was not as yet totally extin-
guished, and, as regarded the scion of the race who
had lately succeeded to his kingdom, "Long may
he reign," was an exclamation of hopeful good-will,
which I more than once heard enunciated by men
who, themselves reduced to bitter poverty, had not
forgotten that they and their forefathers had lived on
" his lordship's " land for generations, and had never
yet been behind-hand with the " rint." But warm
as a heart may be, and loyal with hereditary trust as
well, continued perseverance in wrong-doing will
break the spell at last. When a ruler, be he king or
landlord, persistently hides in distant lands his face
from those who would gladly sun themselves in the
light of a countenance which has hereditary claims

on their affection—when the "payer," he who by
the sweat of his brow earns wherewith to swell the
income of the paid, rarely, if ever comes in contact
with his liege lord, can we wonder (especially in
days such as ours, when the veils which hid alike
their absurdities and their enormities are being
torn aside from habitual abuses) that feudal sentiment should have gradually become extinct, and
that men, and women also should see in those, to
whom their destinies had been in some sort confided,
enemies to be resisted, rather than benefactors to
be cherished.

> " Man, like the gen'rous vine, supported, lives ;
>   The strength he gains is from the embrace he gives.
>   For God and Nature link'd the gen'ral frame
>   And bade Self Love and Social be the same."

CHAPTER VII.

A CANNIBAL COCK.—PADDY SHIEL.—OUR "OUT-DOOR MAN"
AND THE COW.

PADDY SHIEL, our "odd," or, as such necessary
evils are called in Mayo, our "out door man" was
about as perfect a specimen of his class and country
as could well be imagined—spare and rawboned,
and wearing a costume which, since the famine,
had become rare, namely, the blue "tail" coat, ornamented at somewhat distant intervals with tarnished
brass buttons, and the wondrous breeches (probably
heir-looms in the family) open at the knees, and
surmounting home-made woollen stockings—which
in the sporting sketches appended to old world Irish
Tales—represented the typical Hibernian peasant
of the day. Paddy had the misfortune to be a
widower, but his wife before setting forth, which
she had done about three months previously, for
the bourne from which she was never to return,
had taken care to fill to overflowing with help-

less human creatures, the wretched cabin in the
"village beyant" which to them, poor souls, was
"home!" The eldest born of Paddy's numerous
progeny was a girl—a tall good-looking, and as
yet bone-displaying damsel of sixteen, with masses
of magnificent, but totally unkempt, auburn hair,
and the whitest teeth that I ever saw in human
mouth. Not an atom of vanity, nor indeed, as far
as I could discover, of any other feeling, did this
handsome young creature possess. Indolent was
she to a degree that I never remember to have
seen equalled, nor could I in the very slightest
degree make her understand that, her mother being
dead, the care of her young brothers and sisters
naturally devolved upon her.

Well do I remember the day when duty led me
to pay a visit (it was my first initiation into the
mysteries of Irish humble life) to Paddy's cabin.
On my entrance, the smoke from the turf fire,
while it produced, together with other odours,
(whence, proceeding I then knew not) such an
agglomeration of unpleasant smells as never before
had offended my nostrils, prevented me at first
from seeing whether the wretched room—called by
courtesy the kitchen—was, or was not, occupied

by human beings. There was but little light, save that which entered from the open door. The one window was not made to open, and consisted of four panes of glass, brown with the dirt of years, each pane being about six inches square. It was capable of affording neither light nor ventilation; nevertheless, by dint of opening the door to its utmost width, I did at last (my eyes having become accustomed to the smoke and darkness) perceive, in the centre of the room, a wooden cradle; and also it speedily became apparent to me that in that cradle there lay a child, for a whimpering cry suddenly saluted my ears—a cry very opportune, seeing that I was only just in time to prevent a big and doubtless extremely hungry cock from making a carnivorous meal of the helpless infant's eyes. Perched upon the baby's head, the bird with its rapacious beak, had already made a preparatory onslaught, when I suddenly appeared on the scene of action, and drove it, cackling and fluttering, to its stronghold in the family bed place.

"Arrah now, bad cess to it for a bird," was Biddy's sole remark when I told her what I had witnessed; and, judging from the coolness with which she listened to my description, I should not have

been surprised to hear that the pecking out, by a
domestic fowl, of a baby's eyes was an event of
frequent occurrence in "the village."

A craftier individual than plausible Paddy Shiel
it was never my lot to become acquainted with.
It was only by the merest accident that I one day
discovered an ingenious fraud practised by a small
"gossoon" of his, the which fraud had, as we eventually found sufficient reason to believe, been for
a considerable time winked at, if not indeed encouraged by his parent. Amongst the various
duties which devolved upon our retainer that of
milking our solitary cow was one. She was a
tame and gentle beast, and had only recently calved
when we purchased her ; but ere long, and quite
unaccountably, (since "Rosy" did not lack en-
couragement to do her duty as a good milch cow
should), the supply of milk grew short, and neither
Paddy nor any one else could tell the reason why.
At last, and just after it had been decided, that short
as we were of "grass" in our peninsula, another
cow must be added to the establishment, accident,
as I have said, threw a light upon the actual state
of things.

On one singularly fine morning, something—"a

spirit," perhaps, " in my feet," for in the heart of me just then there was but little zeal for enterprise—had

> " Led me—who knows how ? "

to a spot, half hidden amongst some stunted alders—the only signs of vegetation which graced our domain—beneath the shelter of which I saw, resting tranquilly on her side, while she chewed the cud of bovine fancies, our Kerry cow, Rosy!   But she was not alone, for, stretched comfortably, and in loving proximity to her, was Phileen, Paddy's youngest hope but one, who, after the fashion of the calf, from which our milk-giver had been a month before separated, was luxuriously and amply breaking his fast !

As a matter of course, our henchman—whose exclamations of wonder at the *baste's* (bad cess to it !) short-comings had been, during the last fortnight, loud and frequent—vociferously denied all knowledge of his son's delinquencies.   The " I declare to me God," and the " Shure now, I wouldn't be telling your honour a lie ! "—exclamations which habitually precede the utterance, by Irishmen, of the most fearful falsehoods that ever priest took upon himself

---

to wash away,—were in full use on the occasion;
while, as to the "batings" with which the delin-
quent was threatened (but never, to his misfortune,
received), they fell, thick and fast, both about our
ears and his. I may as well here mention that in all
the years during which I sojourned in the country,
no single instance of a child receiving from either
father or mother what may be called salutary punishment ever came to my knowledge.

CHAPTER VIII.

WELL is it for us poor human creatures that we are mentally kept in the dark as to the future, and are ignorant of what a day or an hour may bring forth! It is true that being forewarned is sometimes being forearmed, and that better information concerning the perils which await a man might occasionally give him an opportunity of avoiding them ; but then, on the other hand, what "boding tremblers" would many of us become if more light were thrown upon our individual future, and a "thousand deaths might frequently be died in dying one."

. Perhaps never were four individuals more surely marked for destruction by their enemies than were those who composed an unsuspecting quartet of Saxons travelling, one moonless night in October, along a Connaught mountain road. The party consisted of the

"Captain" and myself, our son, aged ten, and an
English groom, the object of the expedition being
that of inspecting (as had of late been frequently our
wont) the progress made by the workmen, builders,
carpenters, and such like, who had now been for
months employed upon the tenement which was
destined eventually to be our home.

The distance from Westport to the

> "Lake whose gloomy shore
> Skylark never warbled o'er,"

and at the foot of whose "rocks so high and steep"
the grey sandstone walls,—"undressed," to use a
mason's term—of the intensely ugly house, had lately
been surmounted with a roof, is about twenty
English miles, the last half of the journey lying
directly through the heart of the mountains. The
day was, for a wonder, fine ; and our equipage, in-
cluding the pair of spirited mares we drove, was the
same which has already been mentioned on the
occasion of the election day. But not, as then, were
we prepared, either in mind or by firearms, for any
encounter with a foe. The object of the drive was
a thoroughly peaceful one, nor had we at that time
become so imbued with the conviction that the name

of our enemies was Legion, and *therefore* that precautions (as a matter of course) ought never to have been neglected by us.

On we sped—past the squalid town with its numberless beggars—its "objects" vieing in loathsomeness with those which in small Italian towns are apt to crowd round a stranger's carriage—past the pretty wood yclept "Brackloon," wherein self-sown holly trees galore and, in the winter season, the "wily woodcock" do abound, and parallel with whose ivy clothed, grey walls there frets and foams the loveliest of small rivers—a river, the banks of which are thickly fringed with giant specimens of the beautiful Osmunda regalis, whose fronds dip in the rapid current, as, dashing over rocks and boulders, the "Brackloon" winds its restless way towards the sea.

A few miles further on, our course led us through a clean, prosperous, and almost English looking village—not a pretty one it is true, for nature, as well as the art architectural, which is at a low ebb in Mayo, alike forbade that it should be so, but the small houses were both externally and internally clean and neat; more than one boasted of a small flower garden in front of the windows, the which windows were of a fair size, and—no common occurrence in this land—capable of being opened. Take it altogether, no greater contrast could possibly present itself than that which was noticeable between the village of Knappa, with its small church and white parsonage, its tidy children, and its general look of well-to-do-ness, and the typical Irish village with its clusters of hovels, grimy with the dirt of generations, from the doors of which swarms of boys and girls, in rags and filth, rush out, either to beg or to scream defiance at the Saxon as he passes by. Scattered sparsely over the West and South are villages similar to the one that we have just driven through, and the sole reason for the amazing contrast I have alluded to is simply this, that they are "Protestants," and have been so, as the saying here is, "evermore." I do not attempt to account for a fact, which is, well known to all who have travelled, with open eyes and unprejudiced minds, through the country. Let those who are curious in such matters draw their own conclusions from what they must have themselves seen.

And now, trotting gaily onwards, we find ourselves nearing the steep mountain pass known by the name of Shafry. Some years ago no carriage road formed a means of communication between the country we had just driven through and the mountain district, into the dark valleys and desolate *corrals* of which we were shortly about to plunge. Unbroken was then the frowning pile of Shafry, save by its own huge masses of rock, its rapid watercourses, and here and there by an indigenous holly, perchance sown by beak of birds, but how existing in its strength and size appears a mystery, seeing that its roots must be beneath the solid rock, a mass of sandstone which the force of vegetable growth has succeeded in splitting asunder.

It was in the year 1828 that the idea of making a road wide enough to admit of carts passing in single file over the mountain way was first entertained, and the project was carried out with a rapidity that is rare in this country. The inducement for forming this means of communication with theseaboard (namely, the lovely Killery Bay, which for a distance of ten miles runs up from the Atlantic, between steep and arid mountains, towards the lowlands of the Western counties) is to be found in the enormous "takes" of herrings, which, previous to the famine, had brought comparative prosperity to those amongst the peasantry who gained their livelihood by fishing—a prosperity which, with greater facilities of carriage, would, it

was apparent, be largely shared by the proprietors
of the soil, and those whose " rights," dating from
the days when Ireland *was* a persecuted country,
extended to specified distances along the seaboard.
No easy matter was it, however, to put the design
into execution, and great was the cost (£3,000, as I
have heard) which some fifty years ago the Marquis
of Sligo expended on the work; but when all difficulties were overcome, how steep, how narrow, and,
but for the low stone wall which ran along the edge,
how perilous was that toilsome mountain pass ! Comparatively easy, however, as well as free from danger,
must it have been in the days " before the famine "
—days of which we heard so much—when the light
carts, laden with the rich spoils of the sea, conveyed
the packed fish to Westport, and returned empty for
the next night's " take." Comparatively wide also
was the road at that time, for winds and rains had
not loosened the stones and portions of rocks above,
which in *our* time (they having in process of years
rattled down the mountain side) greatly diminished
in many places the original width of the roadway.
It unfortunately happened that precisely where this
narrowing of the road's width was the greatest, the
low parapet wall—sole safeguard against the danger

of a perpendicular descent of upwards of five hundred feet into the valley below—had been totally carried away. By the force of a huge body of rock rolling against it from above, its *débris* were hurled below, where stand in picturesque array the giant boulders, with patient sheep nestling for shelter on their windward side.

At the foot of the mountain, the road over which I have, for reasons that will soon appear, described at some length, all its occupants left the carriage. The ascent and descent to the plain on the further side occupy on an average a little more than an hour of jolting and discomfort, for the road is rarely, if ever, repaired, and to perform the *trajet* on foot is to most persons capable of the exertion infinitely the pleasanter mode of progression. The scenery on either side, whether the eye is lifted to the frowning beetling heights, whence project glossy-leaved hollies safe in their mountain fastnesses from the marauder's hands, or whether the eye rests in a contrary direction, and fixes itself on the distant cloud-capped mountains which line the Connemara road, is, to admirers of the grandly desolate, very striking. Nor close at hand are there wanting objects to admire and interest. On the rocks, and

deeply imbedded in the lime of the old wall (alas!
in *our* mountains lime is not existant!) are ferns in
much variety and tempting profusion, whilst every
where, in each nook and corner, where it can gain
a foothold, and on the surface of rocks, spreading
its thread-like roots in marvellous prodigality, is
that pretty Saxifrage known with us as "London
Pride." But not, as with us, is the one which
grows with such lavish profuseness here a pale, weed-
like looking flower; it is a profusely blossoming
plant of vivid pink, with leaves strong and *fleshy*.
Strange that so it should be in a country which
scarcely knows the sun; stranger, too, perhaps,
that when transplanted into a better soil and more
genial climate, it should lose (which is the case)
its personal advantages, and become, as is the
"London Pride" of England, colourless and poor of
aspect.

But I have, I fear, lingered too long in this description, and must proceed more rapidly to the day's
somewhat eventful end. It had generally been our
habit to return late from such excursions as the one
I am dilating on. The way was a fatiguing one,
the horses needed a lengthened rest, and there was
much at the "New Lodge," as the country people

called the house, to inspect and attend to. On the present occasion, owing to some mistake as to times and seasons, the country boat (a big, unwieldy affair, unboarded as to "flooring," and containing generally a quantity of water between its "knees "), that was usually in readiness to convey us across the small river, steep banked and about a dozen yards wide, that runs between a flat meadow and the portion of land on which the Lodge is built, did not happen to be at our disposal. This caused delay, as did also the rebukings, liberally bestowed, on sundry of the *employés* (the contractor included), who had been signally wanting in their several duties; and the result of all this loitering, and heedlessness of the lapse of time, was that the short October twilight—a twilight shorn of nearly an hour on the lake-shore by reason of the mountain which rises three thousand feet high, like a dark frowning barrier, between the "black" waters, and the setting sun—was drawing to a close ere we set out on our return to Ross. The road, however, to the foot of the mountain, and, indeed, for some third of the way upwards, was tolerably good, and for the rest—well, whilst descending on the far side, it only required care and patient driving. To "feel our way," was as a matter of course requisite, and impediments on the rock side had to be carefully shunned ; nevertheless, to "hug" it in places where the defending wall existed not, and where there was only just space sufficient to admit of our phaeton passing, was absolutely necessary. Unfortunately, these chanced to exist, precisely at the spot where the valley. below was deepest, and the bulwark above absolutely *nil*—a few yards of nearly level road on which horses, eager for home and not carefully held in hand, might be excused for breaking into a trot, the which our steeds, stimulated probably thereto by a very peculiar noise, which in the stillness of the now utterly dark night had broken upon my ears, incontinently did : but the gentle amble in which they had indulged scarcely lasted for ten seconds, for, to our surprise, without touch of bridle, they came to a sudden stand. "The Captain," who brooked neither delay nor disturbance, was about to urge them with the whip, when the groom, who had been walking behind, called out excitedly, as he made his way with difficulty to the horses' heads :—

"For the love of God, sir, don't touch 'em ! Some one has been and put big stones all across the road,

and it's a mercy as we're not all in kingdom come
this night !"

And such in very truth was the case ! On examination we found that a low barricade had been
carefully built right across the road, by would-
be murderers—for by what other name can the perpetrators of such a deed be called, seeing that, had
the horses swerved but a few inches, a certain and a
fearful death to all must have ensued ? The place was
well chosen for the purpose ; in fact, it could not have
been more artfully devised. The stones were all
carefully, even skilfully arrayed, precluding the possibility of their having fallen accidentally from the
mountain side, and doubtless not a few pairs of eyes
were watching our movements from hidden nooks
in the rocks above, eagerly anticipating the moment
'when the enemy, whom their priest had denounced
as accursed, and had therefore doomed (so far as lay
in *his* power) to death, should, with those belonging
to him, be hurled into the fearful eternity whence,
according to their Christian creed, there exists for
heretics no hope either of escape, or mitigation of
punishment.

With a heart full of gratitude for our escape did I
retire to rest that night. That we were not lying at

that moment mangled corpses at the foot of that
awful precipice was indeed a marvel, and a proof to
my mind, amongst many others, that the instincts of
some animals, to wit, horses and dogs, sometimes do
them better service than our boasted "reason" can
always achieve for us. Far better than we were our
steeds cognisant of danger, and to their quick sense
of peril did we owe our escape from this deep-laid
attempt at assassination ; an attempt (as all must I
think admit) which was as cowardly as it was cruel,
for the wretches ran no shadow of risk themselves.
Had they succeeded in their attempt, the crime
would never have been brought home to them ;
whereas when a shot is fired, and a victim is laid
low, there exist on rare occasions some mute
evidences of the crime committed, whilst the per-
petrator thereof incurs, not unfrequently, some risk
either to life or limb from the inborn love of existence, from which few mortals are exempt. The
"mountainy men," so called, and that with evident
contempt by the dwellers in the plains, are noted for
their cowardice, and in after days the remark of "If
they had been Tipperary boys that 'The Captain'
had taken the land of, it's shot he'd ha' been within
the month," was repeated to me as one which the

Mayo boys, honest fellows! had been in the habit
of making to one another, invidiously contrasting, as
it would appear, the pluck and spirit of the Tipperary murderers with the dilatory movements and half-
and-half measures with which the "mountainy men"
of their own country had hitherto carried on the war.

On the occasion of a subsequent visit to the
mountains—a visit which we undertook in the dog-
cart, having for our companion a cheery Hibernian
acquaintance—an accident befell me, the effects of
which I was fated to feel for life. Standing un-
supported, a thoughtless act, upon the seat of the
deep country boat, which, as I have said, was employed to convey us across the river that ran below
the lodge, a sudden gust of wind hurled the boat
against the bank, and threw *me—miserabile dictu*
—heavily upon my knees on to the bare timbers of
the boat. The agony was so great that I fainted
away, and for a while knew nothing of the calamity,
which, in the shape of *breakage*, had befallen my
hapless limbs. Many years have passed since that
unlucky fall, which, after having for many months
absolutely disabled me, left me for life with injured,
and often worse than useless knees. But by far the
most painful portion of what I was, for the nonce,

fated to endure, was the six hours' drive home, over one of the worst roads imaginable, and in a dog-cart, the springs of which were none of the easiest. Everything however comes to an end at last, and so did the tortures which I had then and there to bear. The following morning a surgeon was sent for, but by that time severe inflammation had set in, and there was an end of all hope that while life lasted I should ever enjoy again the full use of my lower limbs.

CHAPTER IX.

LOW RATE OF WAGES.—PEASANT PRIESTHOOD.—TAKING THE
VEIL.—DEAN O'ROURKE.—SISTER MARY IGNATIUS.

ON my becoming somewhat familiar with the
peculiarities of the Western country, few things
struck me as more remarkable than the extremely
small sum which a man could earn by a day's work.
Sixpence and no more was the wage received when
the day's toil was done by those lean, hungry-looking
beings, who leant upon their spades so listlessly, and
looked—which was probably the case—as though
they would not, even if they could, give their poor
strength for next to naught. When I heard, as
I frequently did, those gaunt, enfeebled-looking
labourers (?) abused for their idleness, their do-
nothingness, and their utter want of understanding
as regarded the duties of the employed towards the
employer, I found it impossible not to lift up my
feeble voice in excuse and apology for the working
man. "These people possess," I said, "as 'fine a

sense of justice ' as have those with whom that sense
is synonymous with honour ; and. well they know
that a *real* day's work—aye, even of such work as
their weak hands can do—would be worth to their
employer considerably more than the wretched
wage doled out to them ; no wonder, therefore, that
while they give (as I heard one old peasant say) their
time, of their ' work ' they are very chary." But it
was in vain I remonstrated ; in vain I argued that
higher wages might keep whole families (whose
" support " of course fell upon the rate-payers) out
of the poorhouse ; nothing could move even the
more kindly hearted (and *one* was very tender of
nature) to alter a state of things which had been
" evermore " the same. Innovations were dangerous,
and once they began, who knew where they would
stop ? In short, it was the old story ; payment was
not given from a sense of justice, but, on the contrary, advantage was taken of " need," and the rate
of remuneration was arranged accordingly at what
was considered to be the " market price."

The bitter animosity of the priesthood against the
landlords can be better understood when we remember that, from the hard earnings of the peasantry, are wrung the doles which the clergy claim

as their due. It is hard for a man whose family is as "long and wake" as his means are short, and the will of his priest strong and masterful, to pay his rent and to feed and clothe himself and his belongings; but however difficult poor Paddy may find it to make both ends meet, believe me that the last to suffer from his chronic impecuniosity will be the Father—Flanagan, Kelly, or Bourke—who holds in his hands—according to the fixed belief of these benighted people—the power to bind and to unloose, to doom to eternal tortures or to make happy for ever, the souls of his wretched flock. But "out of nothing, nothing comes," and there is no getting, even by dint of such awful threats as a Roman Catholic priest knows how to hurl at the head of his wretched victim, skin off the surface of a flint, and therefore it was that for the' poverty of their flocks, poverty of which *they* experienced some of the evil, the clergy cursed the landlords in their hearts.

Time was when, amongst the priesthood of the Romish faith in Ireland, there were to be found not only gentlemen, but a goodly sprinkling of the "jolly good fellows," who, in Lever's and Banim's novels, figure as characters to be both laughed with and respected. Those men were not, as is the case now among the Irish priesthood, the sons of small shop-keepers, and of still smaller cotter-tenants. The clergy of days gone by, having for the most part received their education at St. Omer's, had in many cases added the polish of a Frenchman's manners to the natural charm in which a well-born Irish gentleman is rarely deficient. Liberal too were they in their ideas, and genial in their habits—not viewing with distrust and suspicion the Protestant parson who, perhaps, in a neighbouring village, preached to a " few " his comfortless creed, but treating him, as man to man, with courteous good faith, and accepting frankly, as they were freely offered, the hospitalities of the richer folk (whether the said folk were heretic or otherwise), who gladly welcomed to their tables the éducated gentleman whose lot was cast near their abodes. But, as I said before, the race is now extinct, or all but so, and but for my slight acquaintance with Dean O'Rourke, I should never have been able,.even in the faintest degree, to realise what manner of man the priest of other days had been. The last, as I was told, of the old stock was he. Kindly of nature and open of hand, as ready with a racy anecdote as with a cheery song, Dean

O'Rourke was a favourite with both high and low, and proved an ever welcome guest at the houses of the " gintry."

It chanced that, shortly before we took our departure from Ross, the ceremonial of a nun taking the veil was to be celebrated in the Convent of "Our Lady of Mercy" at Westport. With the " Reverend Mother," as the Lady Superioress of the nunnery is called, I had early made, as I hoped, "friends." Of all the women I had ever seen, she was the one who came nearest to my notions of perfection. So tender was her heart, so largely sympathising her nature, so free was she from all the littlenesses which cause us to be contemptible alike to ourselves and to others, that on her small pale face (a face that was not lovely "as some men count beauty," but which possessed nevertheless a charm peculiar to itself,) might be traced even by a " peasant churl," evidences of the pure soul within.

The Reverend Mother, " whose name in the flesh" was Murphy, and whose family, a " good " one (as the saying goes), inhabited County Galway, had kindly invited me to the ceremony, always—to my thinking—a sad one, which immures for life young and attractive girls within the dismal walls of a con-

G

vent. I had paid more than one visit to the nunnery,
of which Sister Mary Ignatius was the guiding spirit.
The "perfect woman" gifted with all the best qualities of her sex, with "reason firm and temperate will,"
appeared to be truly in her rightful place, whilst
watching over the training of orphan children and
bringing up young girls to be domestic servants and
to do their duty in the station of life to which it
had pleased God to call them. And yet what a
narrow life was hers! And I often thought how great
a pity it was that one, so endowed with the rare
power of placing goodness in an attractive light, one
who to "gentleness, *sweetness,* patience," united in
her own person, the

      "Endurance, foresight, strength, and skill,"

which can, on occasion, make of a weak woman a
very tower of strength, had not been granted a
wider field in which to "improve" her "talents."
For in addition to the contractedness of that field,
the time granted for labour therein seemed to be
very short. I had visited the sad looking little
burial ground where, within the Convent walls, the
"brides of Christ" lie buried, and death had without an exception called them early to their rest.

Devoted nurses of the sick are the " sisters," shrink-
ing from no disease, however loathsome or contagious,
and therefore it may be that a large proportion of
those whose deaths I saw recorded, fell on the battle-
fields of duty ; but that there were others, and they
not a few, who perished, simply, yet most miserably,
from inanition—the tedious mental and moral
inanition . of Convent life — is a fact which—on
the testimony of these early graves—I cannot but
believe.

The spacious building was in gala dress that
day, and the Sisters all afoot, and busied in wel-
coming and doing honour to the numerous guests
who had hastened to the " wedding breakfast " of
the bride. The ceremony of taking the veil has
been so often described, that I will pass over its
details in silence, merely remarking that the victim
was only eighteen, rather pretty, and of good birth.
In order to be allowed the privilege of profession, a
postulant for admission must make over a certain
sum of money (the amount has escaped my memory)
to the governing body of the establishment; and, this
done, they one and all devote themselves—heart
and body—to the good of the poor, and the
" making " of their own souls.

The breakfast was served in a large but entirely unadorned upper room, which was well filled with guests, on whom the "Sisters" diligently waited, hurrying round and round the long table, and hospitably pressing tea and coffee, cold meat, and wine upon their assembled visitors. The place of honour next to Dean O'Rourke had been assigned to me, and most entertaining, on this festive occasion, did he prove.

"Ach now, don't be touching the wine at all," he whispered, "shure it's poison, enthirely. They don't know betther, the crathurs—how should they, and they buying the Marsalla at Flanagan's grocery over the way," and he laughed the pleasant, self-satisfied laugh of one who, seeing that he had been "evermore" accustomed to good liquors, understood thoroughly how to choose the good and refuse the evil.

In the middle of the table, and occupying a conspicuous place thereon, was a large wedding cake (bear in mind, Reader, that we were met together to celebrate a "marriage"), and in the centre of that iced and ornamented adjunct of such festivities there quivered on the summit of a spiral spring, a small plaster of Paris figure, representing a full-costumed nun! A painful sight truly to Protestant eyes, and one that shocked every devotional feeling within the heart, for the nun, mounted on her cake, pictured the newly wedded bride, and the joining together of such material emblems with mystic allusions to a purely spiritual union was revolting in the extreme, at least it was so to my feelings.

The task of cutting up the cake devolved upon my neighbour the Dean ; but, after a futile attempt to make an incision in its hard surface, he gave up the attempt in despair, and a laughing nun carried it off for the purpose of stronger hands than the old·man's being employed upon its dismemberment.

" Ach, now," said the Dean, with a roguish glance at the Sister's Irish blue eyes, and speaking, after the fashion of an after-dinner toast, for all the attendant nuns to hear, " I'd be glad if you had all of you a good husband a piece, and shure a better wish I couldn't lave afther me."

" Ach now, Dane, it's yersel as 'ud always be joking," was the smiling remonstrance of more than one of his becoiffed listeners, whilst Dean O'Rourke, with a laugh that shook his well-lined sides, rose from the festal board, and was speedily followed by the remainder of the guests.

Before closing this short account of the Westport
Convent, I may here add that "The Reverend
Mother" did not for many months longer retain
the office, the duties of which she had so well
fulfilled. The order arrived for this gentle Christian
soldier to "move onward." Melbourne had been
selected by the head of her Church as a city in
which a Convent of the Order of Mercy was needed,
and Sister Mary Ignatius, with sixteen of her nuns,
received directions to set forth with the least possible delay to the distant land of which she knew
nothing but the name. A banishment *for life* it
was, from home (the Convent home which she had
loved so well) and from friends and country, but the
brave woman, going forth in her trusting ignorance
across the Tropics to an unknown city, a "city of
strangers" and mayhap of enemies, never trembled
nor flinched. Tearless, when I bade her farewell for
ever, were her soft grey eyes, and the same benign
expression rested on her tender face when I spoke
aloud my wonder at her calmness, her obedience,
and her resignation. Truly no thought of resistance
had ever so much as occurred to her mind. Her
health was delicate, and she might well on that
score have claimed exemption from banishment;

but the "Will of The Church" was to her a law too
sacred and binding for thoughts of self to obtrude
themselves as hindrances to duty. Depart she must;
and therefore she and her followers went forth from
amongst their sisterhood at home without a murmur
or a sigh. Verily, we can scarcely wonder at the
great and growing power of a Church which exacts
and obtains from its followers unflinching obedience
such as this.

Once, and once only, after her arrival in Australia
did I hear from my friend. She wrote from the
"Convent of Our Lady of Mercy," of which she was
about to be named Lady Superior, and sent me an
interesting account of the execution of a "poor
sinner," a murderess, the painful duty of attending
whom during her last moments on the scaffold, had
fallen upon gentle Sister Mary. "The poor woman
was sincerely penitent," wrote the kindly Irishwoman,
"and I trust that her soul is safe with the blessed
Virgin-Mother now." They had been very kindly
treated, according to the pilgrim's account, during
the long voyage, by all on board the ship, and in the
tropics their black serge garments had not greatly
inconvenienced them. "Finally," she wrote, "I bid
you, my kind friend, farewell, and if the prayers of a

poor nun can avail you aught, we shall, when the sorrows of life are over, meet again in the Kingdom of Heaven."

For myself, I sorrowed much, after she went away, that I should "see her face no more;" but for her I could not grieve. She was (speaking with all reverence) about her "Father's business," healing the sick, speaking comfort to the mourner, fighting the battle of life bravely—

> "*Truly* a Christian soldier
> Marching on to war,
> With the Cross of Jesus
> Going on before."

CHAPTER X.

THE month of March preceding the time fixed for our migration mountainwards had been singularly free from rain ; fine "soft" days (to wit, a continuance of gentle "pour," which, known to the Saxon by the name of "Scotch mist," wets the traveller as effectually, though more insidiously, than does the pelting of a heavy shower) had been of rare occurrence. The wind had blown perseveringly from the East, a pleasant "quarter" *here*, reminding one in nothing of the bitter searching cold,

> "Bad for both man and beast,"

which in an English spring calls down upon itself the execrations, both loud and deep, of its countless victims. April had arrived, and still the rain kept off. Turnip growers were in despair, and even graziers were beginning to think that the fine

weather had lasted long enough.   It was, however, a
pleasant season, and one fine day the fancy took us
to drive into the mountain's heart in order to

> "—— visit our snug little farm,
> And see how our stock went on."

It was but little past mid-day, for we had started
early, when we reached the top of Shafry pass, and
commenced our descent on the other side.   The sun
was blazing brightly, and a fresh mild wind was stirring the long grass, called in Mayo, as elsewhere,
sedge, which is useless save for thatching and bedding,
and much of which in early spring is sapless and
withered.   Suddenly our ears were startled by an
unaccustomed and strangely rushing sound, one that
appeared to sweep along the ground, and was clearly,
as it appeared, advancing in our direction.   What
could it be ?   For a few moments we remained lost
in wonder, and then the crackling as of burning
sticks, and the floating away of some sparks which
even the blaze of the sun was powerless to conceal,
revealed to us the truth, namely, that the mountains
were on fire, and that the flames were advancing
with the swiftness of an eagle's flight on either side
the narrow road !   Would they be swept across it,

and thus render our advance difficult, if not impossible, or was the worst evil we had to dread that of the horses taking fright at the approaching flames, and becoming unmanageable in their terror ? Before we had time to take more than a troubled note of the situation, we saw, to our relief, running briskly towards us, some of our own staff of shepherds, (I have forgotten to mention that some short time ere this, our entire system had been changed, and that trusted men from the Highlands of Scotland were now employed as "heads of departments" on the farm,) and they, armed with long sticks, and sickles, were actively employed in endeavouring to stay the progress of the fire. This they did, by making, after the fashion of American woodsmen, clearances in the track of the flames, the which, finding no fuel to feed on, could spread no further. From the Scotchmen we heard that in several other portions of the land, the *sedge* had been simultaneously fired, and that other detachments of their body were busily engaged in preventing the sheep, heavy now in lamb, from being burned alive upon the land,* that being their

* Strong suspicion, afterwards fully confirmed, that the fires were not accidental, was at once aroused by this widely-spread conflagration.

evidently intended fate. By great exertion, and equal readiness of resource, the men at last got the flames under, whilst the number of animals who fell victims to priestly hatred and the blind obedience of the people, was, as I rejoiced to hear, but small.

Soon after this adventure, we, with all our household goods, departed for the

"Land of the mountain and the flood,"

and into the heart of the wilderness which had been made one for us. Previous to that time, *one* who (alone, as I may say) had fully appreciated the high courage of the Saxon emigrant, and who had ever been willing to admit the great advantages which she and hers derived from the enterprise which he had so fearlessly undertaken, bad—after much suffering—been removed from this world of trial. If only health and wealth had been given to her, she would have been as a second Providence to the poor, so bright was the intellect, and so large the heart that now was still for ever.

Heavy was the cloud which, when

"She had gone where all things wise and fair descend,"

rested upon the poor starveling seaport town. The

shops were shut, and very little sound save that of
a wild unearthly " crooning " filled the drear November days and nights whilst " her ladyship was waking."
The sympathiser in their poverty and their woes had
left these poor people, and henceforth—but I will
not anticipate events, contenting myself with saying
that it was not the *small* tenantry alone who had
deep reason to regret the loss of that high-couraged
and true-hearted lady.

As we neared our abiding place, the numbers of
cabins, from which the thatch and roof-timbers had
been removed, increased, and utterly desolate was
the sight which those dry walls—that is, walls built
without lime—presented to the view. I at once
resolved, that as soon as might be, those dismal
yet suggestively eloquent ruins should be levelled
with the ground. The time came, however, when
I grew accustomed to the sight of them, for,
truth to say, there were more painful objects, and
more forlorn associations even than they, with
which it speedily became my lot to make a close
acquaintance.

Practically speaking, the road we travelled ended
at the Atlantic ocean, for the Killery Bay, which lies
at a distance of three English miles from the Lodge,

being broad and necessarily bridgeless, formed almost
as complete a barrier between us and the further
away sou' western lying world, as the " herring pond "
itself. Virtually then we were located in a *cul de sac*,
with precipitous mountains, varying in height from
two to three thousand feet, enclosing us on every
side, and effectually shutting out from our gaze all
objects save themselves—the usually rain-laden sky
above, and the " black lake," lying gloomy and un-
visited by the sun, at the base of the huge *hollow*,
into the heart of which we, its sole human inhabitants, were now making our way.

Some months had elapsed since I had visited the
spot, which, even to tourists who have " toured " it
in the Western Highlands, and who are conversant
with the far famed beauties of the Killery Bay, is as
an almost entirely undiscovered country. And the
reason for this ignorance of our locality is obvious,
seeing that that same bay, along the shores of
which travellers journey from Westport to Clifden,*
cuts them off from all communication with the
grand, cloud-capped mountains, evidently of volcanic
origin, which rise in many a " thunder-splintered

---

* Lately the scene of *religious* rioting.

pinnacle" in the far distance on the County Mayo side.

But, to return to my more immediate subject, namely, our installation in the home which at so heavy a cost of care and money had become our own. The accident to which I have before alluded had, for a lengthened period, rendered it impossible for me to endure the unavoidable bumpings and joggings which a drive over Shafry necessarily entails; and so it fell out that the Lodge had been completed, and made ready for our reception, without my having had an eye (fate having willed it otherwise) to the work which during my absence had been—*left undone.*

The day was a cold one in June, and as we drove along the last four miles of the defile, on which, owing to the height of the mountains, the sun never shines, while the wind cuts through it as through a tunnel, added cloaks were needed to counteract the "biting of the pitiless blast" which even in mid summer assisted the long anticipated mountain mist in its unpleasant task of chilling us to the bone.

At last we have reached the goal! We have been deposited, wrappers and all, in the wet boat, whilst the carriage has returned to the ford of our little river, a distance of some four hundred yards— happily, for the nonce, fordable—whilst we, encumbered with heavy wrappings, make our way upwards on foot to the small space of level ground on which the house in all its isolated dreariness—its unredeemed and native ugliness—frowns darkly.

Kind Readers, (if any such there be among those who may be induced to read this true story of a modern "exile") may I claim your indulgence if now—for the first time after twenty years, during which my lips and pen were sealed on the subject— I record some of the sensations which this introduction to our mountain home called up within me? Silently—for to dire misgivings I gave no outward voice—I put the question, to myself, and that not once, but times uncountable, "How can I bear this life?" and the reply was ever the same, "What has been given you to endure you *must* endure. From the inevitable there is no escape, and surely even here there will be *work* to do— work which will prevent the time from hanging heavily on your hands, for have you not the poor always with you? and in succouring them, in teaching their children, and in endeavouring to make the ignorant and vindictive your friends, you will forget your own trials, your own discontent with the lot which has been assigned to you."

I listened, and I hoped, hoped earnestly, and also, for a short while, strove to find healthy employment in the way that conscience had chalked out. Never however was dream more fallacious—and never were attempts more futile !

How signally I failed—only they, who from experience have gained some faint notion of the hatred which in Western Ireland exists among the Papists towards those of a different creed can thoroughly understand and appreciate.

CHAPTER XI.

OUR SCOTCH STEWARD.—HIS MERITS.—CAPTURE OF AN EAGLE'S
NEST.—A STORM ON DHULOUGH.

A "FINER" man—using the word both in the
American and the English sense of the eulogistic
term—than our new manager could hardly, I think,
be found within the limits of the United Kingdom.
Born and bred in the Lowlands of Scotland, his
father was a "large" and prosperous farmer; whilst
his grandfather had the honour of being the "original" from whom Walter Scott, in his romance of
"Guy Mannering," portrayed the popular and delightful character of Dandie Dinmont. James
Hunter (for such was his name—a name that will
live long in the sanguinary annals of Irish crime)
was about forty years of age, six feet two, at least, in
height, and broad-shouldered and strong in proportion. A good-looking man, besides, he might be
pronounced, for his was one of those frank, cheerful,
honest faces which are in themselves a letter of re-

commendation, and his character and disposition fully answered to his looks. I can see him now before me—him and his magnificent collie, "Turk," the highest bred and wisest of sheep-dogs—and, as they stood together at the first sheep-shearing which I had witnessed upon the farm, I thought that I had never seen a handsomer "pair of friends."

The ceremony of sheep-shearing—that all-important event on a grazing farm—had been again and again postponed, owing to frequently occurring rainy days. Between three and four thousand sheep—I speak now only of the section of the flock which were to be shorn of their fleeces in the immediate neighbourhood of the Lake—had twice gone through the preliminary ceremony of "washing," and still the "fine day" on which the comparative cleanliness of the animals was to be taken advantage of, arrived not! In the meanwhile, the ire, not only of Hunter, but of one among the various Macs from Ross and Inverness-shire, who held authority under him, was greatly excited against a certain sea eagle, a glorious bird, but as arrant a thief as ever "lifted" Highland cattle in the good old days when "might" set "right" at naught. This bird had, according to long respected custom in the family, brought to

H 2

light, in our immediate neighbourhood, and " raised "
well nigh to maturity, a fine family of eaglets. Now,
as is well known to naturalists and others, the eagle
is not only at all times a rapacious creature, but is
besides an exemplary, if not a well-principled parent.
Growing creatures are invariably hungry, and to
satisfy the cravings of nature in their offspring it is
not surprising that the parent birds—father as well
as mother, for there is not a pin to choose between
them—were in the too frequent habit of " reaping
where they had not sown," and " gathering where
they had not strawed." In other words, many were
the young lambs which, in addition to unnumbered
grouse, hares, and other defenceless animals, fell
victims—so averred the Highland herds—to the
greed of these royal marauders ; and the result of
this accusation was, that a raid, or, as I should
rather say, a war of extermination, was to be commenced against them. The campaign was one not
to be lightly undertaken. The enemy was both
powerful and wary, added to which his fortress, that
is to say, the cleft in the rock in which the eyrie had
to be stormed—was frightfully difficult of access,
situated in a gloomy " corry," on one of the steepest
sides of Muilh Rae (which, being interpreted, means

the king of the mountains). Some seven hundred feet of well-nigh perpendicular height intervened between the eagle's nest and the Lake, upon whose dark surface we, that is, the weaker vessels of the party, had taken up our position in a large boat, armed with "field glasses," the better to watch the operations. In all the mountain district round there existed but one well-known and utterly fearless cragsman; and this solitary exception amongst a cowardly race was a reckless fellow who bore the name of Timony, and who had been engaged in our service as a gamekeeper. On this occasion he was told to be in readiness; and, armed with a sharp knife, he, without hesitation, prepared for his dangerous ascent. Already had more than one adventurous spirit, amongst whom was the "Captain," commenced the climb, and with the aid of our good glass we could perceive their motionless figures, "diminished to a span," on certain accessible spots amongst the rocky boulders on the mountain side. He who had approached the nearest to the place where Timony's perilous task began, was the "master" himself. This point was still several hundred feet below the cleft in which the eagles were probably watching our movements. The narrow ledge on which he had taken his stand was covered with short sheep-nibbled grass, and sloped gradually towards the edge of the fearful precipice beneath. With the naked eye nothing of this would have been visible, but with our glasses all became clear, and I shuddered at the peril which more than one actor in the scene was probably about to encounter.

Suddenly, and when our reckless cragsman (he had the character of being what is called " a broth of a boy," but was about as idle and untrustworthy a fellow as could be found in the country), had by slow and cautious degrees surmounted about half of the difficulties that rose above him, a cry suddenly escaped the lips of the two Irishmen who rowed our boat, and one of them, a grave gaunt fellow, called O'Flaherty, exclaimed :

" Ach, the crather! Bedad ! an he's got *his* death, whatever. Bad loock to him."

" Who ? What ?" I exclaimed, as the speaker, apparently but slightly moved by the event which he had announced, quietly plied the oar that kept our little craft from drifting landward, " Has anything happened ? For Heaven's sake, speak."

Thus urged, Mr. O'Flaherty condescended to explain that the "crather" whose death he had so suddenly announced, was *only* a dog, a faithful follower, who sticking as closely as he could to his master's heels, had, through some carelessness or miscalculation, paid with his poor life for the loving temerity he had evinced. The unlucky dog, whose fall headlong to the mountain's base our men had noted, was the property of Timony the climber, and it was not long before I ascertained that the death of the faithful creature was hailed as a boon by these sadly superstitious and imaginative mountaineers. But for his demise—a sacrifice as they believed, to the wrath of the fairies who inhabited the " corry "—another death, that probably of a human being, would, they doubted not, have been the consequence of this invasion of the *fir darrig's* * territory.

Meanwhile, matters on the mountain side were fast progressing. The adventurous Timony had reached the cleft, and, looking in, perceived two fine eaglets, whose plumage rendered them all but ready for flight. Happily for the daring intruder, neither of the parent birds was keeping watch over their progeny. Had even the male (the smaller and less daring of the pair, but which takes its share both of sitting on the eggs, and nourishing the young brood)

---

* Fir darrig—*Anglice*, fairies.

been present, Timony would have found it hard
work to hold his own; even as the case stood, it
needed all his strength and skill to secure the young
birds, and bring them in safety to level ground.

Whilst this feat was being performed, the "Captain" had a very narrow escape of his life. One of
the old birds, wending its way with rapid flight home-
wards, came *almost*·within rifle shot of the grassy
ledge on which *he* stood. To fire was an irresistible
impulse, but in the excitement of the moment, the
slipperiness of the turfy slope was forgotten, and the
adventurous marksman was within a hair's breadth
of being hurled into eternity. But presence of
mind saved him ! Happily the sod was soft, and by
digging his heels firmly into it, foothold was obtained,
and fortunately retained till assistance came in the
shape of a reliable rope, when strong hands lent themselves to the task of drawing upwards to a position of
comparative safety, the "master," of whose imminent
peril and narrow escape I happily knew nothing till
after the short but harrowing crisis was over.

The ultimate fate of the captured eaglets was, to be
securely fastened in a nook within easy reach of their
human enemies. Instinct, it was safely calculated,
would soon lead the parent birds to the spot where

their young had been conveyed, and, whilst minister-
ing to their wants, it would be, and *was* an easy matter
for the Inverness-shire herd (burning with the desire to
avenge the crime of lambecide) to shoot the splendid
pair of eagles dead. A necessary execution, I was
told, but even could I have approved of the deed as
a matter of policy, as a question of sentiment I was
dead against the extermination of these grand
aborigines—these splendid "Arabs of the air." I
loved to watch them in their circling flight on high,
and then the sudden swoop landward to a destined
prey was wondrous in its fell rapidity. Such fearless
creatures, too, they were; one, a splendidly large
specimen of the race, actually pounced upon one of
my own Spanish hens, and that within a hundred
yards of where I stood. But they are not always so
venturesome, for I have seen a small black-faced
sheep effectually keep at bay an eagle which, soaring
within *easy* distance, had evidently an eye to the
small lamb which, unconscious of danger, was dis-
porting itself by its mother's side.

According to the testimony of the very few persons
by whom an eagle's nest has been inspected, the
"remains" of victims to their hunger, which are
there discovered, bear ample testimony to the mis-

chief which they are able to effect. Bones of various
kinds of comparatively small animals lie strewed about,
and the mere description of the scene is, I confess,
sufficient to fire the ardour of a sportsman, and to
cause him to " let loose the dogs of war " upon ·the
thieving *autochthones* of the crags. But experience,
before it was too late, stayed, to my relief, the hand
of the destroyer. Both on our own moors, and on
those of Achill, where the same murderous policy
had prevailed, the grouse, instead of increasing in
numbers with the slaughter of their foes, were found
to sensibly diminish, the truth being that stoats and
weasels, together with such like destroyers of infant
bird life, gained immeasurably by the doing to death
of those (to wit, the eagles), who had in the days of
their strength made many a meal of the vermin
class which did now unduly preponderate. The
result of this conviction was that the royal birds, too
few in numbers, from the first, to do any appreciable
damage amongst the flocks, were thenceforward
spared from "the fierce pursuit of man," the only
created animal, by the way, as says Walter Scott,
who preys upon his own species.

Happily for themselves, eagles have so decided an
objection to feeding upon dead prey that they run

no danger from the strychnine-laden carcases with which the mountains are at certain seasons "poisoned." Their keenness of vision is, as all the world knows, greater than that of any other animal, and it has, I believe, been proved to be a fact that when the eagle itself is so high in air as to be invisible to the eye of man below, the bird can be cognizant of every act and movement on the part of his natural enemy. It is only when the king of birds, after having been guilty of the rashness of descending to terra firma, then and there becomes forgetful of the fact that there is no wind stirring, that he finds himself—after taking a rest—in a " fix." I have watched his impotent attempts to rise, his heavy pinions needing a good supply of air to set them in motion, and have been much amused at his Majesty's false position, but I have also watched him—and it was in truth 'a sight not easily forgotten —with his grand wings extended, and flying at lightning speed before the fierce November gale, chasing a flock of six wild milk-white swans, who, high in air, were speeding across our black lake, driven by stress of weather to seek shelter upon land.

Even without the adjunct of an exciting chase, and when only the war of the elements is visible, a

storm on Dhulough is one of those wondrous spectacles which impress themselves indelibly upon
the memory. An entirely calm day is of rare occurrence on the lake, to which the epithet " black "
is so thoroughly applicable. Its depth, to quote
a countryman's expression, "no man knows;" but
the popular belief is that it has no bottom. Others
are of opinion (though the gloomy waters have never
been sounded), that the height of the surrounding
mountains, namely, from two to three thousand feet,
corresponds with the depth of the water which lies
so cold and dark and dismal at their base. As may
be supposed, many and wild are the superstitious
tales with which Dhulough is connected. Of these
the favourite and most often dwelt upon is the
legend of a certain huge white horse, with flowing
mane and tail, which has been seen by many bound-
ing from the lake, and, as a matter of course, breathing death and destruction to those whose unlucky
stars led them to cross his path.

In the warmest of summer weather, the tempera-
ture of Dhulough is too cold for bathing in it to be
advisable, nor did I ever know the most ardent lover
of outdoor " tubbing " commit himself a second time
to the tender mercies of its chilling current.

CHAPTER XII.

I TAKE TO FLY-FISHING.—HOW AND WHEN TO "STRIKE.

IF during any former period of my life it had been
foretold to me that the time would come when fly-
fishing (a sport which I had always mentally stig-
matised as amongst those which call for "hardness
of heart," in the enjoyers thereof) would become for
me, not only a pastime, but even a pleasant one, I
should have laughed the prophecy to scorn. But who
amongst us can or ought to feel certain of what,
even under *un*altered circumstances, may be his or
her future conduct? There exists also such a thing
as the "law of necessity," and when "needs must" a
Will more powerful than our own often takes the
matter in hand, and "drives" us where we would not.
It was to some such law as this that I succumbed
when I "took" to salmon-fishing. Out-of-door
exercise for a woman whose powers of walking
were extremely limited, there existed in that

mountain desert, none. Riding on horseback, to
which I had all my life been accustomed, was out
of the question, as the only route was up the
steep mountain sides, and along the hard narrow
road which led back to the slightly more civilised
country which we had left behind us. Garden I
had none! Up to our very door reached the un-
cultivated moorland, with its *tussocks* of heather
and bog myrtle, on which, for fear of plunging
into the slough which lay hidden between each
little mound, it was necessary to plant the foot
securely. As to books, well, what with economy
being on this, our second start, the order of the day,
and what with its being scarcely worth while,
"carriage" being difficult and expensive, to provide
intellectual food for *one*, it came to pass that only
books which for years had been my familiar friends
were within my reach. Our nearest neighbours
(indeed, in the country we had no other acquaintance)
lived at the distance of twenty miles, and I had
already begun to perceive that my visits to the
wretched cabins in which our retainers, together with
more than one description of domestic animal,
abided, were as unwelcome to them, as they were distasteful to me. "To be alone," is scarcely less "good"

for woman than it is for man, and "to muse o'er
flood and fell," especially when the rocks are habitually too wet to sit upon, becomes, after a while, and
especially when a state of utter solitude has to be
endured, on an average, five days out of seven, and
from ten to fourteen hours at a stretch, slightly trying to the spirits.   It was under these circumstances,
and seeing that "the rain it rained" (more or less)
"every day" that I made my first essay in the
"gentle" art, one auspicious afternoon in August
(auspicious, inasmuch as, after a heavy flood, salmon
and white trout were certain to have run up the
river to the Lake).   Awkward enough were my preliminary attempts at line throwing! Instead of
letting the strong yet delicate tackle float lightly
upon the breeze, after it had run out from the reel,
and then, soft as thistle down, rest for a second on
the surface of the rippling water, I allowed the
thirty or so yards of line to come tumbling in a
mass (very possibly) before the actual nose of a
hungry salmon, which atrocious deed of course called
down upon my head both reprobation and contempt.
But "practice," although it failed to make me
"perfect" as an angler, nevertheless stood me in
good stead, and not a few big fish, salmon as well as

trout, did I eventually capture. The trout, especially
when they run from four to twelve pounds in weight,
gave by far the better sport. Fishing from a boat
is, I am well aware, greatly looked down upon by experienced salmon fishers, nevertheless, I make bold to
say that the excitement experienced when you feel the
weight of a ten-pound salmon, or it may be of *two*
heavy sea trout, one on the dropper, and the other on
the tail fly, running out your line with a whirl and a
whizz, is not to be despised, albeit felt in a boat.
The rowers are for the moment worked up to a state
of frenzy, so little does it require when *strife* is in
question to stir up the slumbering blood of an Irishman ; and continuous shouts of "pull, Larry," "Aisy
now, Pat," according to the course which the fish, in
its swift rush and struggle for life is taking, pour in
wild confusion from their lips, mingled with exple-
tives which it would be worse than useless to repeat.
And then, when perhaps, after twenty minutes of
"running out" and "reeling up" of the line, the
worn-out prey nears the boat, the excitement on
board reaches its climax, for "whilst there is life,
there is *fear*," and "one struggle more," the last
and the most desperate, may yet give the splendid,
silvery-sided creature, freedom. But it is not to be:

many hands are against him, the line is dexterously
shortened, and, the landing net having been deftly
passed beneath his now motionless body, the capture
is complete. "A fine fish, yer honour,"—"As clane
a salmon as has been caught the year," "Shure, niver
a finer came out o' Dhu*lough*" (great emphasis being
as usual laid upon the last syllable) are amongst the
flattering comments with which my performance is
greeted; but "fine" although he is, I cannot—from
the moment when my victim lies panting, and throwing from moment to moment convulsive "leps," at
the bottom of the boat—endure to look upon him;
and when the *coup de grâce* is to be given, I turn
away my head, and the heavy thud of the execu-
tioner's wooden hammer sends a shiver through my
frame.

I may here, *en passant*, mention that two circumstances connected with fly-fishing have always
afforded me — the first, amusement, the second,
grounds for incredulity. Under the head of the
former, comes the extraordinary weight of the fish
which for some reason or other manage to "get
away," and of the dimensions of which it is of course
utterly impossible to form any adequate idea.
Secondly, as regards the scepticism which "a little

knowledge," begat within my mind (and which in
a tyro was, I suppose, inexcusable), *that* had its
origin in the vexed question of "striking." When
a fish has risen to the fly, and instead of, as in duty
bound, running out a good length of line, makes off
triumphantly, leaving your flies and casting line fluttering in mid-air, the exclamation of those who "know
they are right" invariably is either, "You struck
too soon," or "Why didn't you strike?" Now, seeing that, partly perhaps from frequent inability to
see the "rise," but also from my disbelief in the
possibility of any flexile substance such as "line"
and lissom rod being able to take effect in "striking"
fashion, I never even attempted to perform the feat
at all, it did appear to me, taking into consideration
the fact that *my* failures were not greatly in excess
of those of my scientific lecturers, that the safe
"hooking" of a fish is after all very much an affair
of chance.

CHAPTER XIII.

ONE morning, soon after the grouse season began,
we were startled by the news that two of the most
trustworthy of our Irish hinds—handsome brothers
of the name of Navan—had on the previous night
fallen upon and murdered an old man, whom they
overtook on their return home from B—— Fair.

One of the supposed miscreants had been at once
arrested, whilst the other made his escape, flying for
safety to the fastnesses of his native mountains. On
examination, the following facts were elicited. As
is customary on coming from a fair, the Navans
"had the dhrop taken," and as ill-luck would have
it, they overtook by the way two men, yclept Hanagan, father and son, the younger of whom had so
incurred the wrath of our two herds, that the Navans
had vowed "to their gods" that they would "give
him a bating." Which vow they unfortunately

I 2

kept, but still more unfortunately they not only hit
a good deal harder than they intended, but they bestowed their blows—the night being dark—upon the
wrong man! The cowardly son, whose offence was
the by no means venial one of having " belied " (*id
est,* slandered) Tom Navan to the girl he loved, had,
when he found that matters were going against him,
"skedaddled," leaving his aged, and very much in-
toxicated parent to bear the brunt of the battle.
Little wonder was it, that by that lone road side he
paid the debt of Nature! Medical testimony was at
fault as to whether drunkenness, or blows received
from stout shillelaghs, were the immediate cause of
death, nevertheless a verdict of manslaughter was
pronounced against Pat Navan at Castlebar Assizes,
his punishment being two years' imprisonment;
whilst Tom, the "wanted" man, was—by reason of
his known animosity against the younger Hanagan—
found guilty of murder. To us, both the brothers
came under the head of "losses," for they were
cheerful, open-hearted fellows, glad to be employed, and apparently not greatly under the evil
influence of the priesthood. When the term of his
imprisonment was over, Pat returned to his work,
apparently none the worse for his incarceration ; but

handsome Tom had never the chance of doing a "hand's turn" for us again. For seven long years—during all which time his name was in the "hue and cry," and the police were perpetually on his track—Tom wandered amongst our mountains, a hunted man, saved alike from arrest and starvation by the many "near frinds," country girls amongst the number, who watched over his safety, lodged, and fed him. More than once did I catch a glimpse of the fugitive, who on very rare occasions ventured from the heights on which our hardy black-faced sheep were grazing, to the lowlands which he had once inhabited. On the unintentional crime which he had committed I could not bring myself to look with unforgiving eyes; and when the news came that Tom, after having in woman's clothes made good his escape to Liverpool, had sailed away in safety to New York, we one and all rejoiced that the harassed one had found a rest for the sole of his foot at last.

It was about a fortnight after the arrest of Pat Navan that a singular event, one also of a tragic nature, took place within a mile and a half of the Lodge. On *our* side of the Killery Bay, a small cluster of thatched cabins, together with one slate-roofed building (formerly occupied by the National schoolmaster), raise their unpicturesque heads. In the centre of these hovels, a low, *dry* wall enclosed what was called by courtesy our kitchen-garden, the which consisted of two acres of lately redeemed bog, and was under the immediate charge (as gardener in chief) of a certain unmitigated old rascal (as he afterwards proved), called Paddy Gallagher. The distance from the house of our *Potager* entailed a daily messenger with the vegetables from Bundoragha; but it occasionally happened, when neither wind nor water was favourable for fishing, that " the Captain " would order out the " cair," *on* which national vehicle we drove down, best pace, towards the sea, in order to bring back " green stuff" for the day's dinner. September is in the far West one of the few months during which something like pleasant weather may be hoped for ; and truly, on the day in question, the winds were as hushed, and the sun shone as brightly, as though it were an English July afternoon. We had proceeded along the narrow valley, through which runs the rapid Delphi river, and close to the banks of which our course lay, till we were little more than a quarter of a mile from the village. Suddenly, and as though the noise proceeded from the very bowels of

the earth, the wildest of howls assailed our ears, and
presently some crouching female forms became dimly
visible amongst the long grass that grew beside the
river. It was the first time that the sound of a
genuine Irish *keen* had demonstrated to me of what
Hibernian lungs are capable ; and when Daly, our
coachman, quietly said :   " Bedad, an' there's a
death beyant there," we felt that he had spoken
truly, and hurried him from the driving-seat, in
order that he might ascertain the cause of the
commotion.

In a moment he came running back with the information that one Thady Costello, a " boy " whose
father lived on the other side of the river, had, some
twenty minutes previously, thrown himself naked
into a pool in the stream, at the bottom of which he
lay stiff and stark !

To hurry off Daly and the car with directions to
bring back with him not only our head boatman,
but plenty of ropes and boat-hooks, was the work of
a moment, and during his absence we questioned
one of the women (a *keener* whose wail had for the
moment ceased) regarding the truth of what we
had just heard.

It was but little she had to tell. Biddy Conway

and hersel' were stacking turf on the bog, when,
they, being within a few yards of the river and of
Costello's cabin, heard and saw the father and son
"a' ballyragging" of one another. "Says one 'I will,'
and says the other 'Ye will not have the saddle;' and
thin it was of Katy Doherty they did be spaking.
Says Thady, 'It's to Father Herachty I'll be going,
wid the siller in me fist, and sorra a bit o' delay
will he be making,' and thin the ould man he
fetched Thady a blow on the head, and he widout a
rag on his back threw a lep and fell clane into the
sthrame. Ochone! ochone!"

And so, as usual, the tale was not without a
heroine! The "boy," a fine young fellow and an
only son, had owned, not half an hour before, a passionate loving heart, the which heart had apparently
panted to possess as his own the Katy of his
dreams, and now that heart had ceased to beat.

So much of the story as this might fairly be con-
jectured; but during the short interval (which, however, appeared an age) that elapsed before the return of the car, the mind could dwell on nothing
save the now scarcely possible rescue from drowning
of the immersed lad. In the meanwhile, louder and
shriller still did the voices of the women peal out

their lament; nor did they cease their lamentable howlings when Devanny, our sailor man, who fortunately could to a certain extent both dive and swim, plunged into the deep pool near to which the "boy" had taken his spring. From off a big boulder stone he had jumped, and at the bottom of that pool poor Thady lay a corpse !

The bringing of the body to the surface was a work of time and difficulty, and, when achieved, it was abundantly clear that even had the means wherewith to attempt resuscitation been at hand, to employ them would have been utterly useless. So Thady's "remains" were taken back to his father's cabin to be duly and honourably waked. "Lashings of tay" and whisky were consumed on the occasion, and whilst the corpse of the dead man, with face uncovered, lay in the midst of the "company," songs of the liveliest description were sung cheerily during the orgies of the night. The atmosphere breathed during these orgies—an atmosphere thick with smoke and bad tobacco—is better imagined than described.

The cause of Thady's death remained a mystery, for the County Coroner, though twice written to concerning the catastrophe, *never called an In-*

quest, and we were therefore left to form our own opinions on the subject.

It appeared that the poor young fellow had for some months past been " courting" the pretty peasant girl whose name I have already mentioned. On *his* side mercenary feelings existed not, but in the West of Ireland, as elsewhere, the parents of the young people, having their senses about them, insist on *something* being exchanged between the parties more tangible and lasting than that evanescent thing called " Love."

Now amongst the peculiarities of the Far West, the existence therein of an individual known and acknowledged as a professional match-maker is not the least remarkable. The duties of the man thus singularly recognised as a necessity are by no means confined to the introducing to one another of the supposed eligible " parties." A kind of itinerant individual is he—a gossip of the first water—who receives a warm welcome, together with his " support" and a night's lodging, in any house at the door of which it may suit his purpose to knock. On him devolves the (so to speak) drawing up of the marriage settlements—in other words, it is Peter O'Shane who, acting as " go-between," arranges with the "high contracting parties" the amount of worldly goods which the "frinds" on either side are to produce on the occasion. With the priest also who has to perform the ceremony Peter finds himself not seldom officially in communication, for the Father—who generally knows to a fraction how much each individual of his flock is "worth"—is sometimes given (of course in the interests of "the Church,") to the sin of extortion, and cruelly refuses to make the loving couple happy until a certain sum has been paid down. But the most fruitful causes of delay in the coupling together of boys and girls, whose united ages frequently do not exceed five and thirty years, are to be found in the extraordinary avarice and greed of the "parties" themselves. The haggling and bargaining between the respective families sometimes continues for a whole year, while in the case of Thady Costello, the question as to whether or not an old saddle was to be thrown in as part of the *fiancée's dot* had been, for seven long weeks, a vexed one.

But whether or not the lad, who, according to his unhappy mother's story, had stripped himself that warm September day to bathe, had been, as one of the howling women averred, knocked into the water by his father's blow, or whether he had, then and there, by his own act and deed been drowned, was a mystery which, seeing that the "authorities" never troubled their heads about the matter, was not even attempted to be cleared up.

It did not take us long to make up our minds that in the "remote, unfriended, melancholy" Mayo mountains, the arm of the law—long and far-reaching as it is popularly supposed to be—is little in the habit of making its power felt. Till our advent, the Priests had been the ruling spirits, and that they would not see their influence lessened, without vigorous efforts to retain it, was a fact of which we had already had more than sufficient proof.

CHAPTER XIV.

To " attend Divine Service " was for us an affair
of considerable difficulty. During the comparatively
brief season of prosperity, and also of belief in its
success, of which the then much talked-about "Achill
Mission" could boast, subscriptions for the building
of Protestant churches in the West flowed in merrily
from England. The wonderful reports printed and
published by the enthusiastic and well-intentioned
supporters of the proselytising movement, in regard
to the numbers of those who had abjured the errors
of their forefathers and become converts to Protestantism, were received with a pleasing credulity, not
only by the frequenters of Exeter Hall, but by the
immensely numerous class of excellent persons who,
in the United Kingdom, are ever on the watch to
echo the " No Popery " cry, and to spread aloft the
banner of the Reformed Faith.

Of their abundance, the rich, and of their *mites*, the comparatively poor, gave in the good cause cheerfully; their liberality being none the less welcome or useful, for the reason that it had its source as much in Christian hate as in the love from which all good gifts should spring. Churches, in which the numerous " brands '' mercifully "plucked from the burning" could (without the con- comitants of idols in wood and stone) worship in their new Faith, sprang up as if by magic in all directions, and amongst the evidences of zeal, which in Connemara were remarkable, I may mention a building of tolerable dimensions, subscribed for by ardent anti-papists at home, who opened their purse- strings widely in the firm but mistaken belief that there were, in the neighbourhood, Converts enough to more than fill it.

Beautifully situated at a distance of two miles from the head of the Killery Bay, this little church had for its "incumbent" a clergyman ap- pointed by, and receiving his salary from, the "Church Mission Society," the funds of which had unfortu- nately been of late considerably diminished through the misconduct and subsequent misappropriation of moneys committed to his care by another Reverend

gentleman connected with the Achill Mission. Ill-paid
enough were the Protestant clergy who undertook
the difficult as well as delicate work of carrying on
in the Far West the work of proselytising; but,
speaking from my own experience, I feel forced to
confess that, limited as was the pay dealt out to
them, it was, in almost every instance which came
under my notice, more than the services of those
employed were worth. Not that the young parsons,
who, fresh from Trinity College, Dublin, had brought
but little "knowledge," and a still smaller amount
of *tact* and good manners to the work in hand, were
deficient in *zeal;* for they possessed, on the contrary,
more than enough of that often dangerous quality;
"sons of thunder," as a rule, were they, Boanerges,
gifted with a controversial spirit so fiery that to
provoke their priestly opponents to the bitterest
wrath appeared to be the chief if not the only
object which they had in view. The virtues of
"Patience, Meekness, Temperance," virtues which,
if they might not have gone far in the "making"
of Converts, would at least, by their exercise, have
secured for the "mission" clergy a certain amount
of respect, were conspicuous by their absence; and,
instead, violence of language, insults not only to

the priests in person, but to the Religion they pro-
fessed, were amongst the favourite and usual means
by which these very objectionable missionaries hoped
and believed that they would accomplish the ends
they had in view.

The distance both by sea and land which separated
us from the Aasleigh Church to which I have just
alluded, and the duty of providing some facilities for
the attending at Divine Service not only of ourselves and household, but of the rather considerable
number of Protestant retainers whom we had enticed
from their native land, induced us to request that a
small National School-house, slate-roofed, and of
conventicle appearance (which " since the famine "
had been entirely "closed to the public") might
be utilized for our benefit. A small expenditure
only was needed to give its interior the semblance
of a chapel. A few benches, a hassock or two, and a
desk, whence a very red-haired young zealot, whose
surplice was usually both unwashed and in holes,
did, on every Sunday afternoon (the building having
been duly licensed by the Bishop), air his eloquence
in violent tirades against the Religion he detested.
Such were amongst the means employed by us to
metamorphose into a church the ugly square tene-

ment in which, when Bundoragha was a populous village, the children of "a bold (?) peasantry" now to "kinder shores" departed, learned, in days gone by, their A B C's.

Our congregation was a small one. On a tract of land consisting of some 64,000 acres, many of the Highland shepherds, (who one and all were of the Presbyterian persuasion, and therefore somewhat lukewarm as regarded attendance at Episcopal Services) lived at so great a distance from Bundoragha that the power of swelling our congregational numbers was practically denied them. On an average "the two or three who were gathered together" might be calculated as twelve souls (a greater number, by the way, than the morning attendance at the "regular" Aasleigh Church; and much in excess of many protestant congregations throughout Ireland, before the passing of the Disestablishment Bill. Our Boanerges (also the Aasleigh minister), whose name for obvious reasons I suppress, was never deterred—so much justice I gladly render him—by any amount of bad weather from the duty of attacking, on Sunday afternoons, by means of a good rattling controversial Sermon, the errors and the "idolatries" of the Church of Rome.

K

Assuredly the Anathemas which he poured forth, and the provocations to strife that he offered, were enough to arouse, even in the meek, a contentious and a revengeful spirit. In very truth they came not amongst us in the spirit of Peace, but in that of "War to the knife." On one occasion, this stalwart defender of the Faith, did, in the course of some twenty minutes or so, speak of the Blessed Virgin as "a sinful, unrighteous woman;" of the Cross as "a blasphemous emblem;" and of Roman Catholics, both generally and individually, as hopelessly doomed (they being liars and idolaters) to everlasting burning.

Can we wonder that when the gauntlet was thus violently thrown down—when strewed by the road-side were frequently found printed papers containing the bitterest abuse and ridicule of the Priests—when "Scripture Readers," mission-sent, forced themselves into the cabins, and *obliged* the inmates, however averse to the infliction, to listen to the Word of God;—can we wonder, I repeat, that under such and many other provocations to wrath, the "clairgy" should have accepted the challenge, and done on their side fierce battle in their cause?

Amongst the few Irish who occasionally attended our Service was a somewhat repulsive looking man, around whose head was fastened a broad black bandage. On making enquiry, we found that the individual, once a Scripture Reader, had so greatly (in the heyday of his fervour) exasperated the bigoted dwellers in a lonely cabin who refused to listen to the voice of the charmer, that they then and there—horrible to relate—cut off his ears! To my thinking, albeit I am one of those who to make one *true* convert would gladly "compass sea and land," the act of encouraging Roman Catholics to read a book forbidden to them, is on the part of Protestants *wrong*. Methinks that every rightly judging man or woman amongst those who deem it a sacred duty to obey the Priests that are set in authority over them must, in his or her heart, blame the would-be converter who begins his work by inculcating the sin of disobedience; and therefore it was that I, incurring thereby much blame from zealous acquaintances at home, never either encouraged or exhorted our people to read indiscriminately the scriptures. Indeed my *entire* disbelief in the existence of any genuine case of an adult papist having—to use a term common in the West—conscientiously "jumped," would alone have constrained me, whilst talking to the ignorant peasantry on the all important subject

of their "souls," to use the utmost caution on this
momentous question. Without touching on the
"points of faith" for which from time immemorial
"graceless zealots" have fought and perished, it was
not difficult, without greatly shocking their prejudices, to here and there throw in a word calculated
not only to enlighten *them*, but to weaken the
prestige of their priestly tyrants. It was something
gained to convince even one amongst them that I,
a Protestant, believed in a merciful Saviour, and
recognised the Holy Virgin as "Blessed amongst
women." They had been told the contrary by
Fathers "Pat" and "Pether," whose object it is to
lower all heretics in their eyes, and when the poor
creatures discovered that in their Faith I could see
much that was beautiful and true, something akin
to sympathy was established between us: the fine
edge of the wedge had been inserted, and I could
venture upon mild "chaffings" as to priestly thrall,
and the utter absurdities which their Riv'rences
(generally for the purpose of extorting money) too
often frighten their ignorant flocks into believing.

CHAPTER XV.

WE FIND IT HARD TO KEEP OUR OWN.—AN ACT OF CELTIC
REVENGE.

BY slow degrees an air of somewhat improved
civilization began to manifest itself around us. A
" dry " wall (one which, being so, stood in constant
need of repair, and propping up) had been built
at the height of some few hundred feet on the
face of the mountain yclept Glenumra, which rose
precipitously at our *back*. The enclosure formed by
this wall, which extended to a distance of about
two hundred yards in either direction from the
house, had been thickly planted with trees a foot
high, principally the commoner kinds of firs. In
the immediate vicinity of the house, one of Glenumra's giant shoulders afforded some protection from
the whirling currents of air, which in mountainous
districts are far more destructive to vegetable life
than are even far stronger blasts when they are blown
fairly in the face and from one direction. Screened

then by this friendly projection, the small trees near to the house grew and flourished mightily, affording us, in the course of a very few years, both beauty and shelter, whilst those that were exposed to the whirl of the "powers of air" dragged on a miserable existence, and were, at the end of twenty years, scarcely an inch taller than when their roots first laid hold of the turfy tussocks on which ling and heather stoutly maintained their primeval rights of ownership.

One of the first and most necessary acts of amelioration had been the erection of a wooden bridge across the deep but narrow stream which, running below the house, emptied itself at a short distance westward into the lake. Not only to ourselves and to our extremely rare visitors was the existence of the bridge a boon and a convenience, for previous to its spanning the river "travellers" to and from "the West" (a generic term for the neighbourhood of the small town of Louisberg) had no resource when arriving at the broad and usually shallow mouth of the stream save that of fording it. It not unfrequently, however, happened that the water was too high to admit of its being crossed in safety; and in consequence there was nothing for it but to *wait* till such time as, the floods having subsided, both foot

and horseman could "go on their way rejoicing."
Most willingly was permission given by us that on
such special occasions the new bridge might be made
use of, but it very soon came to pass that the ford-
way was almost entirely abandoned, and that *our*
" way " ceased altogether to be a private one. In
many respects this encroachment on our rights was
the cause of both annoyance and damage. Tribes of
beggars, *certain* of being housed for the night in some
of the cabins " beyant," would come across the bridge,
avoiding the ford altogether, and not only hang about
the stables, but, creeping up the back way to the
kitchen entrance, would, after uttering the usual
exordium of " I'm expecting me dinner," squat there
till the hunger, which often did not exist, had been
relieved. Another consequence (but that was an
affair of later days) was the cutting down and carrying off in the dark nights of big branches of quickly
grown and beautiful hollies. Grand shillelaghs I
could believe that they would make, but that was no
consolation to us who had for years lovingly watched
their growth, and I confess to having entertained,
when one wet August morning I witnessed the de-
vastation, an ardent desire to see proper punishment
inflicted on the perpetrators.

It was "the pilgrims" who had done the deed!
Pilgrims to St. Patrick's Holy Well :—a shrine
which it behoves all good "Catholics" to visit
during the month of August, and get gloriously
tipsy at. Far a-field, from County Galway and
from Clare, did the "Faithful" troop; most of them,
the women especially, on foot, while two, and sometimes three men held on to one another on the back
of a willing, but ill-fed "horse baste." All were in
holiday garb, the women with bright coloured shawls
and petticoats, but bare-footed. In consequence of
the want of shoes during the time when the ford
had of necessity to be crossed, the females of the
party were often largely employed in carrying their
males—*proh pudor !*—over dry shod upon their
shoulders. A narrow, and in many places extremely
perilous bridle-path, led them a distance of some
dozen miles to the Well, where whisky and devotion
held their united sway. It was on the return of the
excited revellers, after a three days' orgie, that the
damage to my shrubs was generally effected. We
could hear them in the dead of night as they
came whooping and galloping along, not necessarily
bent on mischief, but brimful of *spirits,* and of a
comfortably secure sense that the burden of their

sins had been removed from their backs, and that they might " go and sin " *again*.

I have hitherto alluded only to comparatively trivial misdeeds, of which the votaries of the patron saint were guilty; but I must, ere winding up this chapter, refer to a crime perpetrated within a few yards of our coachman's house by other and far worse delinquents. Amongst the comparatively few crimes to which the western peasantry are addicted, that of sheep stealing had been for many a day not only one of the most frequently committed, but the most difficult either to bring home or to punish. In the mountain districts intermarriages between near relations are a fruitful source not only of the concealment of crime, but of the vast amount both of scrofulous disorders, idiotcy, and madness which exists in the country. Of the latter evils this is, however, no time to speak, whilst of the mischievous results, as regards crime, of the close clanship which marrying "in and in" produces, it would be difficult to say too much. Previous to our occupation of the land, the small tenants, whether they were behindhand in their "rints" or otherwise, had been to a great extent tacitly permitted to allow their "stock," —consisting probably of a few half-starved Irish

sheep, and a cow or two which at night shared the
"childre's" bed—to have, as it is called, the "run
of the mountains." Now the boundaries of our
"take" were adjacent in more than one direction
to lands that were inhabited by "unfriendly tribes."
Very far from "scientific" was the "frontier" which
divided us from predatory hordes, that is to say,
from the wretchedly poor peasants (also tenants of
an absentee landlord), whose sheep, for the most
part scabby, habitually trespassed on our mountains,
whilst their owners, by whom the four-footed delinquents were *driven* to wrong-doing, showed but
small respect for the distinction between *meum* and
tuum as regarded *our* stock.

Several times had our Scotchmen tracked the
"lifted" animals to the cabins of the marauders
(a service of no little danger), and with the aid of
the Westport police had even caused the guilty
parties to be brought to trial. But conviction even
of the comparatively mild offence of trespassing
was in almost every instance unattainable. The
"feeling" was at that time so strong against the
"usurping Saxon" who had covered, with beasts of
the field, land, "every rood" of which, according to
the "Nation" and other such newspapers would have

"maintained a man," that juries cared not to venture their lives (the same being precious in their sight), by finding a verdict of "guilty," either against a trespasser or a sheep-stealer.

Once, and once only was the crime of sheep-stealing so thoroughly proved against some men of known bad characters, that not only were our branded animals restored to us, but the thieves were sentenced to imprisonment, for what period, however, I do not at present remember. And bitter cause had we to regret that twelve "intelligent men" had at last done their duty.

Great was the rejoicing when Jamie McLeod, the Inverness-shire man who had given evidence at Castlebar Assizes against the culprits, returned with the intelligence that justice had at length been obtained, and that "the two Kearneys" had been sent to prison.

"My certie, but they've got it now, whatever," said McLeod as he stood gravely, bonnet in hand, at the hall door, and then "good nights" were exchanged, and we were left to congratulate one another on the event, anticipating the *certainty* that this conviction, better late than never, would strike terror into the heart of the marauders, and greatly diminish if not entirely prevent the recurrence of such lawless acts.

Alas! our triumph was of short duration. Early in the morning the dire news spread that poisoned "*male*" had been forced between the bars of the kennel, and that every dog therein was dead! Six *bodies* in all they were, stark and swollen—poor dear creatures! Fine red Irish setters, whose honest eyes had been wont to greet—as it is only in the power of dogs' eyes to do—my coming, lay stretched upon the kennel floor—

"Sleeping the sleep that knows no waking."

It was only the day before that two valuable pointers had arrived from England, and they also were numbered with the slain!

That this wholesale slaughter was an act of revenge for the incarceration of the Kearneys, committed by the "near frinds" of the convicted sheep-stealers, no one for a moment doubted. They had a "strong back" in "the West," and the outrage, perpetrated at our very stable-door, must have been the act of men who were returning after the Assizes to their homes, "Louisberg way." The ford, owing to recent rains, was hardly safe to cross, therefore

the wretches must have taken advantage of our
bridge to administer the poison with which they
had come prepared. Well greased meal, mingled
with a quantity of arsenic, was found sticking to the
bars of the kennel; but all attempts to obtain proof
against the doers of the deed proved futile. From
long experience of the Irish character, I think myself justified in saying that the majority of the
people take a positive pleasure in the mere act of
concealing crime, and thus defying laws which it is
their nature (simply because they *are* laws) to hate.

I may as well here remark that neither trespassing
nor sheep-stealing were one whit diminished by the
punishment which drew upon us the murder of our
dogs; and it may not be altogether unworthy of note
to add that, during the twenty years we passed in
Ireland, the above is the only instance which occurred
of a " cause " being decided in our favour.

CHAPTER XVI.

THE farm had been by Hunter divided into
separate districts, each one of which was overlooked
by a Scotchman; and amongst the nine Highlanders
whom we had brought from their native land to
one that was in every respect unsuited to them
was a shrewd but taciturn fellow of the name of
Shaw. He lived on a distant portion of the property, and nearer to the "plains" than most of
our Highland retainers. His family, "long and
wake" when he arrived, had increased yearly since
he came to the West. Report said that he was
making money fast, and there were not a few
amongst the sworn enemies of his race who averred
that the "Scatchman" Shaw, not content with his
lawful gains (in common with the rest of his
countrymen he was allowed the "grass" of forty
sheep and four cows) was having recourse to ille-

gitimate means wherewith to increase his wealth.
To none of the many stories told by the "foe" did
we lend a believing ear. That John Shaw was
laying by money was probable, but then the pay of
working men should—in my opinion—be sufficient
to enable them (if careful and prudent) to provide
for their old age and helplessness. The workhouse,
as a last refuge after a life of toil, is a dismal
look-out, and a large family must be a constant
spur and incentive to "turn pennies" as profitably
as may be. Shaw's "district" was nearly the best
upon the farm; he had chief charge of the large
stock of West Highland cattle—about two hundred
in number—which increased and multiplied on his
district; consequently, had he not been "a good man
and true," he might easily have filled his pockets
at our expense. An especially useful man, and one
not easily replaced, was he considered by his em-
ployers; and consequently, one dark, moonless night,
a party of ruffians (acting on the belief that by
means of intimidation they might drive us from
the country) fired three shots into John Shaw's
house. The room into which the cowardly rascals
fired through the window was that in which Shaw's
children lay asleep. Happily the aim was just an

inch too high; had it not been so, nothing could have saved the slumbering bairns from being found in the morning " all dead corpses ! "

Immediately after this outrage, which had followed on threatening letters addressed to ourselves, a party of police were, on application, sent by the Lord Lieutenant, not only for our protection, but to make strict search for the guilty men, who, it is scarcely necessary to add, were never brought to justice. Shaw, a man of weak constitution and of timorous nature, suffered greatly in nerves after the occurrence, and, two years later, turned his back upon a country of which he justly remarked that " a mon's life is not his own in it, whatever."

It was some little time previous to Shaw's departure, that we finally disembarrassed ourselves of a species of "stock," against which, though great profits were at one time expected, Shaw, as well as all the Scotchmen, had from the first set their faces. The "stock" to which I allude was *equine*, an idea having early taken possession of the master's" mind that to improve the breed of Connemara ponies, by a judicious admixture of "blood" from England, was a measure fraught with advantages of more kinds than one. The project was carried into execution almost as soon as formed. Mares, to the number of nearly a hundred, were, irrespective of age, shape, and of their previous histories, by degrees picked up, and a sire which, if not precisely "desert bred," united in his own magnificent person the defects as well as beauties of the Arab race, made his appearance—to the terror of the peaceable villagers—at Bundoragha. In process of time, slight, long-legged foals, the advent of each one of which caused a thrill of excitement in the household, were given birth to on a soil, and in a climate that could hardly be called congenial to their constitutions. Still it was wonderful that exposure to rain and cold, to fierce gales of wind, and, last, not least, to the evil of lying on wet bog land, should not early have thinned their numbers; but it did not. Probably the hardy constitutions of their mothers stood them in good stead, for at one time, what with mares and yearlings, there could not have been much fewer than a couple of hundred "horse bastes," as the country people say, upon the land. But the foals, take them altogether, were weedy, weakly animals. They were utterly deficient in bone, "took after" their Arab pro-

L

genitor in lowness of shoulder, and, in very many
cases, far more nearly resembled their elder half-
brothers and sisters, than the Arab parent to whom
they owed their birth. The once hardy and handsome race of purely bred Connemara ponies is
almost extinct ; could any such be found, a mixed
breed between carefully chosen mares, and a
high-actioned, well-shouldered " Suffolk Punch "
might prove a profitable one. The " long, wake,
four-legged family" which we had introduced to the
mountains were of far too delicate constitution to
flourish there ; moreover, horses, as is well known,
spoil even more grass than they eat, one consequence of which peculiarity was that the poor
animals were constantly being driven off the better
kind of pasture, which the herdsmen—being human
—naturally desired to keep for their own sheep, or
—*possibly*—for ours.

One of the many offences against established
rules was the habit, freely indulged in by the
Irish herds, of harbouring, not only more beasts, but
a different species of animal, from that which was
allowed them—(generally speaking) *in* their cabins.
Two cows, and a calf till it was three months old,
they were permitted to keep ; but of pigs and geese,

not one : the reason of this prohibition being that
both do injury to the grazing. Sheep will not feed
where geese have "fouled" the land, and pigs are,
excepting to Irish eyes, dirty and objectionable
everywhere. As most of the cabins inhabited by
the subordinate herds were situated "on the bog,"
and at some distance · from a solid pathway, it
followed that to secrete · from view the forbidden
"crathurs" was not a very difficult task to an
ingenious and mendacious people,. During daylight,
and when those "having authority" were conjec-
tured to be elsewhere, *soi-disant* calves, but which
were likely to produce, as heifers, a good round price
at some approaching Fairs, were carefully kept in-
doors, as were also the geese and grunters. Grass
was. cut for their "support," and when night fell,
and deeds of darkness could be committed undiscovered, the animals were turned out to shift
for themselves till dawn of day. To what extent
(if at all) our "heads of departments" winked (either
from fear, or from love of gain) at these and similar
ill deeds, can now never be known. Liberal as were
their salaries, it certainly required a greater amount
of courage than they were paid for possessing, to
do their duty thoroughly. Had the hated "Scatch-

men " gone on the system of telling all they knew, few, as well as evil, would, I ween, have been the days of their pilgrimage in "proclaimed" County Mayo.

CHAPTER XVII.

As I have already, I think, hinted, my "calls"
upon our ever complaining neighbours were evidently as far as possible from being welcome. Invitation to enter I never—excepting in cases of ill-
ness—received, and I attribute this lukewarmness as
much to priestly influence and to the hatred of race
as to the cause above mentioned, namely, that, in the
dark, smoky, unsavoury cabins of these "schaming,"
ingenious people, there was generally something
which they deemed it necessary to conceal from
prying eyes. Most, if not all of those benevolent
persons who have endeavoured to improve the
dwelling-places of the cottagers in Ireland, can bear
witness to the tacit though unspoken antagonism
which the latter have uniformly displayed when it has
been a question of cleansing the augean stable, and
letting in light and air upon its hidden mysteries.

To any windows larger than a foot square, and especially to windows that will open, they have a very decided objection. The peat-generated smoke may either remain within the walls, or escape where it will. The hole at the top is, of course, the legitimate mode of exit, but still more *convanient* are the gaps between the rough stones of which the "dhry" walls are built, and also the space beneath the sodden and often dripping sedge with which the black and decaying timbers of the roof are thatched. Dismal sights, especially to English eyes, are these miserable hovels, and the more so as in one, or at most in two rooms of these too suggestive tenements, whole families are usually at night herded together; whilst pigs and poultry, to say nothing of a cow and calf, combine to produce an atmosphere which it is more expedient to imagine than to realise.

It is a shameful but none the less a true fact, that the description given by Spenser, more than two centuries ago, of the Irish cabins precisely tallies with what they are now. Houses with "one smoak," and with the "swine," etc., etc., living with the family, are amongst the many details which the poet and statesman of Queen Elizabeth's day has handed down

to posterity. Strange that in Queen Victoria's reign
the two accounts should so well agree! Strange,
and most discreditable, not only to our country
generally, but to such individuals as might, if they
chose, ameliorate the evil. Far am I from assert-
ing that there did not, at the time of which I write,
exist, even in the Far West, well-intentioned landlords who, according to their lights, endeavoured to
introduce amongst their small tenantry wholesome
and sanitary reforms. For instance, certain laws
(the penalty for breaking which was that awful one of
"eviction") had been framed, and in more than one
instance had, I need not add, been enforced. At
stated times both the exterior and interior of the
cabins were to be whitewashed by the occupant ; no
"lodgers" were to be housed, and the "live
stock" were on no account to find shelter with the
family. Domiciliary visits were periodically paid by
the under-bailiffs—men formerly known by the obnoxious name of "drivers"—in order to ascertain
that all was as it should be; and, as may be supposed, the affection of the tenant for his landlord
was not increased thereby. The Irish are, as all the
world knows, a shrewd and not easily deceived
people. In the rules thus laid down, ostensibly for

their benefit—rules which were enforced, so to speak, at the point of the bayonet—they could only trace, on the part of the landlords who lived in another land and evinced no individual sympathy with either them or their needs, that *love of power* and rule which is one of the most frequent causes of injury to the human race.

The coercion of fear, long exercised, cannot fail to lower the character, and sap to its foundations all that it might once have contained of honourable and good ; and it was by this fear, the fear of losing their " holdings," that the landlords retained their power over the tenants' votes. To grant a lease was to make a man independent, and it was also to deprive the Protestant owners of the soil of an arm against the encroachments of the " clergy " (a fact in which lies one of the landlord's valid reasons for refusing leases). In a contested election the yearly tenant was to a certain extent a " chattel ; " a black mark was placed against his name if he refused to do his owner's bidding, and eviction was certain to follow swiftly on the refusal. On the other hand, should the man whose vote was so precious to both sides be firmly fixed upon his dearly loved " holding," both " Father Pat " and he could snap their fingers at the enemy, the relations between whom and the rebellious *fief* (relations which ought to be replete with mutual goodwill, respect, and, may I not be allowed to add, *obligation?*) would become, as a matter of course, even less friendly than they had been before.

But to return to the absence of sympathy and, I may almost add, the disregard of human health and life, to which, in the dealings of the so-called rich with the Far West poor, I have already alluded. The rates paid for the maintenance of these unhappy people in the Unions, and above all for their sanitary condition, are tremendously high; why, then, may I be allowed to ask, was, and I fear *is*, the beautifully situated town of Westport year after year a prey to the ravages of typhoid fever? An anecdote was once told me—and it was repeated by one well worthy of trust—which in itself speaks volumes in support of my assertion that sympathy between rich and poor is here, as elsewhere, wanting.

In a Western town, fever of a putrid type was raging. The poor-house was overflowing with patients, and the number of the deaths therein was increasing. It was the day on which the poor-law guardians met, and the "doctor" of the *Union*, a tender-hearted and liberal man, rose up, and said:

"Shure, gentlemen, the only way to save some of the crathurs is to allow them a dhrop of port. It's the stringth they want to have put into them, for they're jist—I declare to me God—as wake as wather, and it isn't work'us tay as will put them on their legs again."

"Well, afther I said the words" (I am quoting the doctor's own account of the matter now) "the gentlemen they had a gran' talking amongst themselves. There was some for the poor crathers getting a better physic than ever came out o' my shop, but there was more agin their having it; and one of the guardians—and he with a big rent-roll, and niver a chick nor a child to spend it on—he outs wid his gold pencil-case, and makes what he calls a calkerlation. The price of a parish funeral he learns in a jiffey, and the cost of a bottle of port is well-nigh as aisy to know; so says he, afther he has summed up the account,—and I'm not telling ye a lie, but his face was as serious as if he'd been a Methody preacher,—'It costs more to bury them, so they'd betther have the wine.'"

"Surely," I said, "he must have been joking. Melancholy as the subject was, I cannot think that he really made it a serious matter of calculation."

"Troth, an' he did.   And, as a practical man, which the gentleman prides himsel' on being, I don't doubt that he thinks hissel' in the right.   I've known him more than once to do a kind thing though, all the same; but, ye see, the landlords they can't git over the feeling that the poor are as much beneath them as the dirt, and to be as aisily trodden down.   They have an idea that, because the land is theirs, they are a kind o' kings, and can make what laws they please.   Bedad, and there was one o' them who, whiniver a man said something in the 'office' (that's where the rints are paid) that the landlord didn't think was true, shure he was down upon the crathur, with a thundhering 'That's a lie, me man.   Pay down five shillings at onest.'"

"And did the men actually pay it ?   By what right could the money be possibly demanded ?"

"Troth, an' by none at all; but they knew betther, the poor divils, than to object; so they out wid their money-bags, and the fifteen pounds which my lord himself said was got that way, went, I believe, to the employing of some labourers on a road that was wanted.   Bedad," the doctor added with a laugh, "if it's *lies* throughout the counthry, that the landlord I tell ye of, would be putting a tax on, it's a richer

man than the Queen herself, let alone the Lord
Liftenant of Oireland, that he'd be the day."

Regard for my interlocutor's feelings as an
Irishman would, I hope, have prevented my making
any allusion to a National vice, from which no class,
however elevated, is — in the Emerald Isle—
altogether exempt. That this is so, I have heard
regretfully acknowledged by more than one honourable and truthful Irish gentleman. Account for
the fact they could not, but none the less true is it
that, according to the statement of one of these
candid children of the soil, before he had been
(after an absence in England or elsewhere) a year
in his native land, he found himself displaying
an indifference to truth that was positively alarming.
I have listened to more than one hypothesis as
regards the remarkable and world-known fact,
that the Irish are, far and away, one of the most
"lying" people on the face of the earth; and I see
no reason to deviate from my own notions formed
long ago on the subject. Excitable natures, worked
upon by the passion of fear, and imaginative ones,
allowed to run riot in the mazes that are of their
own creating, are alarmingly near the slender
barrier that separates exaggeration from downright

untruth. Errors as well as crimes are not only
epidemic, but are capable of becoming chronic disorders; and when we add to this disgraceful fact
the teaching of the priesthood, which is—as all
know who are acquainted with the subject—so well
calculated to encourage the belief that falsehood is a
venial offence, that is to say (according to their published catechism), no crime at all, who can wonder at
the existence here—as a national blot—of the vice to
which, as the Psalmist has declared, every individual
man is more or less addicted.

Whilst writing of the little value which, in the
Wild West is—by "poor law guardians," and also by
those who might through their influence bring about
a better state of things—often set upon the physical
well-being of the poor—I may as well in this place
state some of the crying grievances to which the
dwellers in the Far West *were,* and it is to be feared
are still exposed, as regards medical aid in case of
sickness or accidents.   Under the most favourable
circumstances, "help" could not be obtained under an
interval of time varying from nine to twelve hours;
and when obtained—ah ! well-a-day for the patient !
—inasmuch as the " doctor," probably an ignorant
tyro, and not unfrequently primed with the *dhrop,*

had never in his possession any medicines save those
which, having been originally of inferior quality,
had been rendered by length of years perfectly
devoid of curative properties. As in the case of the
Mission clergy, efficient doctors will not, for the sake
of an infinitesimally small salary, bury themselves in
a dreary

"Land of flood and fell,"

in which they have no individual interests. Certain
reports, corroborated by results, as to the medicines
employed, having come accidentally to my ears, a
great compassion for the neglected sick took possession of my mind, and I mentally decided that,
while I had the means to succour and to save, the
poor people should not be left to the tender mercies
of the "guardians" who were appointed by law to
look after them in their needs.

"Necessity is the mother of invention." That it
made of me a "medicine woman," and a greatly
trusted one, there can be no doubt; and by the aid of
good physic, as well as good food—when needed—the
reputation I in a short time achieved was marvellous.
The simple creatures—mothers who had vainly
striven to induce their over-indulged screaming
offspring to swallow the thick, nauseous dose of stale

rhubarb and magnesia which, at the "Dispensary"
some twenty miles away, had been dealt out to
them, gazed in open-mouthed astonishment at the
" miracle " which the tiniest pinch of tasteless
powder had produced upon the teething child; and,
on the strength of some—to their thinking—almost
supernatural cures, my practice speedily grew to be
far more extended than it was profitable.   And yet,
it is perhaps wrong as well as untrue to make the last
assertion, for I have since had occasion to know that,
but for the use which the country people made of
me (one which caused them never to scruple sending at the deadest hour of the night, to request my
attendance on the sick or the dying), the often
threatened event which would have rid the country of
the intruder might with small delay have taken place.

A more cowardly people, whether in " small"
health, or in real sickness, than were my patients, it
would be difficult to conceive.   The men—no uncommon physiological fact—far exceeded the women
both in impatience of bodily pain, and in the fear of
what, "after death," the "clairgy" might do, or
cause to be done unto them.   I have known the
father of a family brought to such an abject condition by the application of a mild mustard poultice on

his chest that his howls could be heard at the distance of a hundred yards. Shame he evidently felt none, although *I* was present during the infliction, and I have been amused by seeing the bite of a leech produce effects equally marvellous.

The most common malady met with here is dyspepsia. A man who gorges himself with "pratees biled wid the stone in em " is likely enough to suffer from oppression in the stomach ; but, frequently recurring as were the symptoms (namely— " a loomp—saving yer honour's prisence—on me hart,") which betrayed the existence in the patient of a slight attack of indigestion, no sooner did pain begin to make itself felt, than the interesting invalid, with groanings loud and piteous, sent off *first* for the priest, and then for the doctor—that is to say—for me. This, I own, was exasperating ; and, notwithstanding my determination not to interfere, even in the minutest degree, between the priests and their benighted flocks, I made it a *sine quâ non* that my services, and not Father Pat's, should be the *first* called in. In cases of fever, a man's pulse is not likely to be lowered by threats of being metamorphosed in another world into goats, reptiles, and especially into *hares,* of

which animal the mountain peasantry have such a
superstitious dread that the chance meeting of one
by the way is sufficient to make a man turn back
home again, however important his business abroad
may have been, " for shure he wouldn't be having
the loock to sell his baste at the fair the day."

But to return to my invalids, and to their blind
faith in the virtues—as regarded the healing both
of soul and body—which the people believed their
spiritual father to possess. To him and to the
Virgin were all my *best* cures attributed. *My* vigils
and anxieties (for sorely did I often feel the heavy
responsibility which the obstinate refusal of the
people to see "the parish doctor" entailed upon me)
went absolutely for nothing, a result of my frequent
visits, which was (to say nothing of the fact that
"accident" sometimes played successfully into the
"Father's" hands) certainly aggravating. Gratitude, however, being a quality which I never expected to find in the Irish character, I was scarcely
disappointed when its total absence was thus practically brought home to me.

CHAPTER XVIII.

DIFFICULTIES OF SEAL FISHING.—THE BEAUTIES OF KILLERY
BAY DESCRIBED.

AMONGST the treats which we were enabled to
offer to such chance visitors (few and far between,
unfortunately) as fate, or our landlord's kindness
caused to make occasional "sunshine in our shady
place," I must not omit to mention the trips, either
in a four or a six-oared boat to the mouth of the
Killery Bay.

It was only in the "dull season," to wit, before
grouse shooting had commenced, and when, owing
to the rare absence of rain, the rivers were not in
order for fishing, that these, to me, delightful
pastimes could be indulged in ; and in proportion
to their infrequency were they appreciated and
enjoyed.

To "sail" down the bay (a distance of about
eight miles, to a spot near its mouth, where, in the
reign of Queen Elizabeth, a Spanish man-of-war,

laden with gold, went down for aye, "with all her crew complete,") was a proceeding which always filled me with the direst alarm. It is not to be denied that a " Hookah "—the sailing vessel of the country—is a safe description of craft enough; but when rigged English fashion, that is, with plenty of canvas spread, the Hookah is as little to be trusted as is any other small sailing vessel with which it has been my lot to become acquainted. And, as regards the dangers that attend its navigation, the Bay *is* practically a lake. On either shore, and descending almost precipitously to the water's edge, are situated high mountains, causing currents of wind as dangerous as any that in Cumberland and Westmoreland have hurled unwary landsmen to a watery grave; whilst the suddenness of the squalls, as they rush upon the little craft, is a thing to be seen rather than imagined. The chances are a hundred to one against the wind proving favourable for both the down and the up voyage. To "tack," although the grand water-way is in no place less than a mile broad, and is so deep that a line of battle-ship can from end to end anchor within a foot of the shore, is a proceeding fraught with difficulty and danger; *danger* from which I alone shrank; but when the

question was one of personal discomfort to all, and
also of returning home, it might be, long after the
important hour of dinner had sped by, then opinion
veered round to my side, and instead of the Hookah,
the services of the "long boat" were called into
requisition.

Infinitely varied are the objects, both animate
and inanimate, which at every moment meet the
eye during a "row" from Bundoragha down to the
broad Atlantic. On both sides rise the mountains,
with their rugged faces heather-clothed, and with
their steep sides ornamented at frequent intervals
by rushing watercourses, narrow, silvery ribbon-
like lines, edged with ferns, and rendered tortuous
by huge masses of rock, from which jut self-sown
hollies and dwarf oaks. Suddenly, as the boatmen
are pulling slowly along near the shore, there is
heard a startling noise, a splash as of a submerged
body, and there is a cry of "The otter!" and we
remember that we have approached the deep cave
in which the amphibious creatures whose capture
it is so difficult to effect, are known to have "evermore" lived and flourished. As a matter of course,
the otter escapes unscathed, but astern of the boat
there has been noticed for some time a seal, its

round black head being alone visible above the
water; and this only at intervals, the suddenness of
these creatures' disappearance being usually com-
mensurate with that of their first apparition in the
wake of a passing craft.

The exclamation of "A sale, yer honour!" from
the lips of the six men whose faces are turned south-
ward, is, of course, the signal for attack. Rifles
lying "convanient" are loaded, the rowers are
warned, on their lives, to keep steady, and above
all to be silent, for the seal *must*, it is computed,
the next time he rises to breathe, find himself within
killing distance of the boat. In my intense anxiety
for the creature's escape, my eyes are fixed almost
unconsciously on the water, which is (or the intended
victim would not have been out, on what the Irish
call a *schokaraun*) as smooth as a mill-pond. On a
sudden, within fifty yards of us, I see, standing out,
dark and shining, in the middle of a broad stripe of
sun-illumined waters, the slowly advancing head at
which two murderous weapons are levelled. There
is a loud report, both rifles having been fired at
once, their aim (the attacking "parties" being
practised marksmen) having, as all on board believed,
taken effect upon the living target, which had ad-

vanced with such calm and touching trustfulness within their weapons' range. That the " sale " was dead—" Kilt enthirely, bad cess to it "—all with one accord declared. The *bodies* of these animals are, however, in consequence of their immediate sinking, very seldom seen again. It is, nevertheless, I suppose, a satisfaction to their destroyers to remember that the salmon—indeed, the whole finny tribe—have an enemy the less when a seal has paid the debt of nature. This satisfaction was not, however, in the case of which I write, destined to be experienced by my companions ; for, lo and behold ! half a minute afterwards there was again to be seen, though at a considerable distance northwards, the same round black head, now rising and anon sinking, which had aroused against it the " killing " instincts of its human foes.

It was " very surprising "—" How could the brute have escaped ? " so ran the regretful comments of the Saxon sportsmen ; whilst the Celts, and amongst their numbers *I* enrolled myself, secretly rejoiced that victory had not, in this instance, been to the strong. From no compassionate motives, however, such as mine, did the satisfaction of the Irish arise, but simply for the reason that the ignorant amongst them entertain a firm belief that at the period of

the Great Flood the souls of the majority, for whom
no ark of refuge was provided, entered into the
bodies of seals, whose descendants, the "sales" of
the present day, naturally are.

Although the flesh of the seal is far from being
either unpleasant to the taste or, in the Bible signi-
fication of the words, "bad for food," yet, during the
famine, and when the pangs of hunger were most
severely felt, nothing could induce the "mountainy
men" of the West to assuage the cravings of nature
by making a meal of seal's flesh. There is certainly
something strangely human (of humanity, that is,
in its least brutish form) in the mild, appealing expression of this—it is said—music-loving creature's
eyes. Seals are easily tamed, and many have been
known to evince a faithfulness of friendship towards a
kindly master, which I, speaking from sad experience,
have, as a rule, looked for in vain amongst my kind.

It must not be for a moment imagined that seals
and otters are the only animals which during our
run down the Killery we have an opportunity of
depriving of the life that God had given them to
enjoy. There are ugly dark green cormorants, their
long awkward bodies motionless as if carved in stone
—watching from their vantage-ground on a rock for

the fish on which it is their purpose incontinently to
dart; whilst in another direction, thousands of screaming gulls are hovering over the mackerel or herring
fry with which the Bay is teeming. No easy thing is
it to " bag " either one of these, or a specimen of the
restless " seapye," as the creature darts and dives,
now upon, and now under its native element. Millions of these birds inhabit the islands, large as well
as small, that lie at the entrance of the bay, and
extend for a considerable distance—to wit, Boffin
and Clare Islands—into the Atlantic. It is, I think,
a pretty fancy on the part of the Western peasantry
that if your pillow should chance to be made of
feathers from a wild-bird's wing or body, sleep will
refuse to visit your eyelids. The idea is one which
must, I think, have originated in the wondrous restlessness of these pilgrims of the air, which are ever
and always on the wing. So like white spirits of the
chainless winds do the snowy seagulls—in their aërial
flight—appear, that one feels inclined to address them
in the words of Shelley to the skylark—

" Birds *you* never were."

But, " bide a wee," as the Scotch say. Watch
the movements of the thronging multitudes when

one of their number has been wounded, and lies helpless and at their mercy. See how they flock about him, fighting, screaming for a portion of his poor mangled, and still breathing body; and then say whether the birds, whose outward seeming is so white and pure, do not contain within their breasts some of the instincts of a man.

At the entrance of the bay at last! How freshly comes the breeze across the broad Atlantic, and how tremendous is the dash of waves, which, even on a comparatively calm day, tells of the mighty impediments to navigation which Nature has placed at the mouth of this wondrous harbour. In almost any other nation in the world, such a harbour as the Killery Bay affords, would, in spite of natural obstacles, have made that nation's fortune; but in *poor* Ireland its advantages are—excepting for the lovers of the picturesque—almost entirely thrown away.

On the north, or Mayo shore of the Killeries, the mountains, from Bundoragha to the sands of Agoul, and indeed for a considerable distance beyond, are included in the very extensive acreage of which *we* held the leases from the proprietors of the soil. Those small white dots which we saw grazing perilously near the edge of jutting precipices, were

our black-faced sheep, while the thatched cabins
nestling in their utter loneliness amongst the "*folds
of the overlapping hills*," were tenanted by our
herds. What a life, and what a "raising," as I could
not but tell myself, was the one to which the children
born and bred in such a solitude were doomed!
Road to such hovels there existed none. Education
of any kind was as entirely out of the question as it
was sorely needed; and the little savages, for such
in truth they were, "wild on the *mountains* ran,"
their minds as vacant as their bodies were dirty and
unclothed.

Cases of sheep-stealing on the part of the still
wilder and more reckless aborigines of the opposite
shore, were frequently reported. The "Galway boys"
were known to be adepts at the crime, and certainly
the long line of shore on which the sheep habitually
grazed was almost wholly defenceless. Nothing
could seem easier than for the wild, half-naked,
and often half-starving marauders to come across
in the dead of the night, and triumphantly carry
off, in their big fishing-boats, the coveted prey.
That some sheep were, either with or without the
connivance of the Irish herds, thus captured is
highly probable, and that the losses thus incurred

were not more considerable was doubtless in part
owing to the activity and swiftness of foot of the
Highland sheep, for their wiry little legs could take
them into " situations," where the coveted animals
were for the moment safe from human pursuit.

Any prospect more beautiful than that which
meets the eye from the summit of a *quasi* island
adjoining the sands of Agoul can hardly be con-
ceived.   To land on this spot, which is—only at low
water—a peninsula—is extremely difficult, and this,
even in calm weather, owing to the dash of the
waves, and the exceeding slipperiness of the rocks ;
but, once landed, once seated on the dry short grass
—by sheep be-nibbled—with which its surface is
covered, methinks that few would grudge even a
slight wetting when the object to be obtained is
so amply remunerative.

I have already, I think, said that during our ten
months yearly residence therein, the inhabitants of
" the Lodge," were not only deprived of a considerable
portion of daylight, but also of the glorious spectacle
which " the god of gladness shedding his parting
smile" over the land, affords.   *Here,* however, when
between us and America stretched only the pathless
expanse of ocean, ample though rare amends for the

privation were accorded us. "A thing of beauty" is
—as I need hardly quote—"a joy for ever;" but
things of beauty, even though they may be splendid
Atlantic sunsets, may be described too often, and
therefore,—with the exception of saying that not the
least beautiful portion of the sight was the reflection,
"deeply purpled" on the opposite mountains, of the
rich vermilion in which the god of day sank to
rest, (the "golden path of rays" *striping* in fantastic
lines its brilliant surface),—I shall forbear from
any lengthened description of a sunset on the Far
Western coast.

The sands at Agoul are simply perfect—so soft, so
extensive, and so dry. Literally swarming with
rabbits are the hillocks of sand, clothed with the long
grass which only flourishes in such soil as these
prolific creatures have chosen to burrow in. The
ground is, the people here aver, honeycombed by
the thousand *conies* who in their subterranean gal-
leries almost defy pursuit.

The row home, which—after catching "whiting
poults" from the rocks, and taking up lobster pots—
is commenced, does not yield in charm to the voyage down ; that is to say, provided there is a moon,
and that the weather "holds up." Far loftier than

in daylight, stand forth against the sky the giant heights of Mhuilrea. Over all Nature there is cast a shadowy gloom. Hollows are intensified into mysterious caverns, and

.   " On the jag of a mountain crag "

there rises, in the pale moonlight, a huge mass of rock which so closely resembles an ancient ruin, that it recalls to the memory old world Castles on the Rhine, gazed at and admired years ago, when

" Life went a maying
With Nature, Hope and Poesy,
And I was young ! "

CHAPTER XIX.

IT is, I think, only fair to mention that amongst
the crimes and vices to which human nature is
liable, that of burglary, or stealing from a dwelling
house, is but little known in the Far West. The
teaching of the priests may in some measure account for this happy exception, for the sin of theft
is, in a little book entitled "What every Christian
ought to know," and published by authority of
Cardinal Cullen, dealt with, and explained after a
fashion so mystifying, that persons who from necessity or inclination are led to the breaking of the
Eighth Commandment may well be excused for
knowing in reality very little about the matter.
"If," says the voice of the cardinal in this small
book, "you steal a *little*, the sin is a venial one;
but if you steal a little from several persons so
that the whole amounts to a good deal, the sin is
a mortal one." The following was amongst the

sentences contained in an edition of the same catechism, which was afterwards suppressed, destroyed, and bought up: "To steal from a heretic is no sin at all !" A startling enunciation certainly, and one which ought perhaps to have taught us the wisdom of employing bolts and bars, warning bells, and iron shutters, in order to "confound the knavish tricks" of our priest-taught neighbours. We had, however, recourse to nothing of the kind; visitors, whether on predatory or amicable purpose bent, we neither expected nor received "calls" from, and consequently neither bell nor knocker adorned our entrance door.

To those amongst my readers who deem the sight, at breakfast, of a morning paper a necessity of existence, and to whom many "posts" a day are among its habitual concomitants, it may cause some surprise to hear that *our* letters were, during eighteen years, brought to us daily by a "boy," whose walk, for the attainment of that end, extended over no less a distance than forty miles. Two of the sons of our Bundoragha labourers were "told off" for the postal service, their duty being to take the "bag" in the morning, and bring it back at (say seven) at night. On reaching the Lodge, thirty-seven miles had been accomplished, and as will easily be believed, the offer of remaining for the night in good, dry quarters was invariably pressed upon our hardy post-lad's acceptance (when according to custom the rain had soaked through his 'waterproof (?), and the searching winds that hold high festival in Glenumra's valley had chilled him through and through), but invariably the invitation was given in vain. After eating his supper (a good *meat* meal, to which variety of diet we partly attributed the fact that in all the country round there were no such stalwart lads as those who "ran the post,") off set the young fellow, like a giant refreshed, for his three miles' journey home. The pay of the boys, who when they had grown to man's estate were superseded by younger lads, was sixteen pence a day, double the wages, with us, of a full-grown man. The same messenger never performed the duty two days running; but, if a longer period than usual elapsed between the journeys, they used to complain of being "shtiff" in their limbs!

Besides the daily wage of eightpence when at work, our labourers lived rent-free, had the "grass of a cow," and were allowed to cut as much turf, for their own use, as they chose. In consideration of these privileges, they were bound, when required, to work for us for the pay which I have just named.

No long period after our installation in the mountains had elapsed, when the necessity of making, at a cost of some £700, a road across five miles of shaking bog, became apparent. Communication between our district, buried as it was in the heart of the hills, and the high road, leading from Westport to Clifden, might almost be said not to exist, and that such a state of things could not be allowed to continue, became evident to the "home authorities." So the carriage - road leading to the highway was commenced, and, what was more surprising, was in process of time finished. Two wooden suspension-bridges were built, the largest of which had so perilously wide a span, that when a carriage of any kind passed over it, even at a slow walk, the boards of the flooring would spring up and down, after a fashion which to a nervous traveller was not a little agitating. Fifty feet beneath, there surged over big boulders the turbid waters of the Errive river, and right glad I confess was I, when, after having closed my eyes during the not frequent *trajet*, I found myself and my belongings safe once more on *terra firma*.

N

But, as if to prove to us how vain are the attempts of mortals to " ensure success," scarcely had this expensive work been concluded when one stormy night, a night that followed upon days of unceasing and heavy rain, a tremendous flood, rushing from the upper country, so swelled the waters of the river, that their force, after uprooting trees innumerable in pretty Errive wood, carried away, as if it had been a wooden toy, the apparently solid, three-arched structure, built of big blocks of stone, the picturesque beauty of which had been the admiration of many a tourist.

By this event our new carriage-road was, *as* a carriage road, rendered useless. Like most rivers that are fed by streams running from the mountains' sides, the Errive, at the spot where the bridge had stood, was fordable only on rare occasions by foot passengers, and it will hardly, perhaps, be thought possible—taking into consideration that the way thus rendered all but impassable was a "public one," and, as I said before, led directly from one considerable town to another—that between two and three years elapsed before the bridge was replaced, and the high road once more rendered efficient for the service of the public. I confess to being ignorant of the nature of the disputes to which might be attributed a delay that, I venture to say, could hardly, under similar circumstances, have occurred in any other civilised country. To *heavy* rate-payers, such as we were, it certainly seemed hard that two of the commonest advantages derived from such payment were denied to us. Access to medical aid, and the power of moving without difficulty or danger along the roadway, were privileges which were apparently not reckoned as amongst our rightful claims.

Had it not been for a melancholy event which long after the carrying away of Errive Bridge occurred at the place where it had stood, it is, methinks, doubtful whether a still longer time would not have elapsed before commencing the highly necessary task of replacing it. This event was no other than the death by drowning of the popular, warm-hearted landlady of the Westport Hotel. The poor woman, whose energy and concern for the interests of her large family were unceasing, had taken fright at the sudden departure of a creditor, whose route had been traced to Clifden ; and, therefore, Mrs. Daly, late on one dark, squally afternoon, set forth "on her own cair" in pursuit of the fugitive. On arriving at the ford, night had closed in, the river was "high," and a certain Johnny Macdonnell, one of the most honest of our Irish herds, whose house was close to the stream, and who had, it was said, realised a small fortune by carrying tourists and others over the ford, entreated Mrs. Daly not to attempt the crossing; but all in vain. With an escaping debtor in front, and with the possible loss of forty pounds on her mind, no amount of threatened danger was able to turn the spirited and ill-fated woman from her purpose.

"The night, saving yer honour's prisence, was dark as the divil's mouth" (I quote Johnny's own words when he came the next morning to give us an account of the dreadful accident) "and the river raging like mad. Says I, 'You'll be kilt enthirely, marm, if ye thry to crass the night.' 'But,' says she, 'if I don't, the blayguard will be away to Galway and off by the stamer to Ameriky,' and wid dat she ordhers the boy to dhrive on, he and she and the governiss all on the cair togither. Down the road they goes, and that was the last, yer honour, as I saw on 'em all alive agin. The noise of the wathers dhrownded the rattle of the wheels, but they was gone, whativer; and I stood and listened, for divil a bit of anything could I see. In a minute—it warn't more, for I wouldn't tell yer honour a lie—who should come up from the wather but Tom Kaine, the cair-driver. He was a'most dead, the crathur, wid the fright and the cold, but I could make out that the cair was upset, and that the two ladies were in the wather. There was none but him and me to help ; but the governiss, she got out someways herself. Through the dark night we searched high and low for Mrs. Daly, but sorra a bit could we see of her till morning came ; and then, by gorra, there she was a-standing upright, as you may say, near the bank, wid the wather up to her waist."

"And quite dead, of course ! Poor woman ! what a terrible end to come to, and all for the chance of saving forty pounds."

"Troth, thin, yer honour, but forty pounds is a good loomp of money," suggested Johnny, who, dismal as was the occasion, gave vent to one of the loud laughs to which he was subject, disclosing, as he did so, a formidable expanse of bright red gum, and yellow teeth galore. The ugliest " boy " " in the three counties " was Johnny, but being a " snoog man," and very careful of his money, he had contrived to secure to himself as a wife the prettiest girl for many miles about. Shrewd as any of the hated

"Scatchmen," and eke as plodding was Johnny, but
he had a kind heart withal, and so, suddenly recover-
ing from his attack of merriment, he said sadly—

"We got her out o' the river, the poor crathur,
and the dead horse as well; and the son, Mr. John
Daly, he brought the covered chay to take the body
back to Westport. Shure, as she sat in it in her
bonnet, sorra a one would belave but what she was
alive the day. It's a gran funeral they will be
having; for Mrs. Daly was good both to rich and
poor, and there's many a one that will be wanting
a male will be wishing of her back agin to give it
'em.''

CHAPTER XX.

EFFECTS OF SOLITUDE.—WHAT AN ATLANTIC GALE ON SHORE
COULD DO.—DESCRIPTION OF MY GARDEN.

UNFORTUNATELY the two years during which communication with our kind had, owing to the non-
rebuilding of Errive bridge, become more than ever
a work of difficulty, were also years than which none
more persistently rainy could be remembered by the
"oldest inhabitant." The Shafry Road had fallen
into such a ruinous condition as to be well nigh
impassable for a carriage, and neither county nor
barony would defray the cost of its repair. The
sense of imprisonment (whether the condition actually
exists, or is only due either to a weakened condition
of nerves, or to the misfortune of a *lively* imagination), is at all times oppressive. The *cri de la
nature*, "I can't get out," whether uttered by a
"starling" or a "Prince," is one that awakens a
sympathetic chord in most human breasts; and the
monotony carried to extreme, which is generally

a concomitant of captivity, does not tend to render the "cry" less plaintive. In this rain-visited home of ours on which—

> "Not a setting beam could glow
> Within the dark ravine below,"

"*les jours se suivaient, et se ressemblaient* comme deux gouttes d'eau." Day after day, as regularly as morning broke, the same scene presented itself, or rather the absence of scene ; for the rain, like a huge white curtain, hid even the outlines of the mountains from our view. Alternations, and very frequent ones, there were of storms and whirlwinds. There were days together when the lake, lashed into fury, threw up waterspouts of spray to the height of several hundred feet, and when the thunder of the tempest caused an uproar so loud and stunning that often, without a considerable raising of the voice, conversation within the walls of the house became irksome, whilst to face such a gale in any sort of vehicle was a work of danger. In order to give some idea of the force of the wind which, in wild currents such as I have witnessed in no other part of the world, raged round our dwelling—I may mention that on one occasion a solid coach-house door which, having been taken off its hinges, lay flat on the meadow opposite the stables, was by sheer force of the gale lifted to a height of some sixty yards into the air, and after having been there mercilessly whirled about, was carried across the river, and flung down, high and dry upon the opposite bank.

The increase of poverty on estates adjacent to our landlord's was very marked during those two years of almost perpetual bad weather. Fuel was almost entirely wanting, and the ravages of the potato disease caused more than one starving woman to bring dying children to our door for succour.

In other and more genial climes—

> " Seasons return ; but not to me returned
> Day, or the sweet approach of even or of morn,
> Or sight of vernal bloom, or Summer's rose,
> Or human face divine ;
> But cloud instead, and ever-during dark
> Surrounded me.   From the cheerful ways of men
> I was cut off."

A not very exaggerated statement is the above, of the circumstances which attended existence at Dhulough. The " seasons," singular and paradoxical as the assertion may sound, did *not*, definitely at least, return there ; for very rarely was there a day of the year in which a fire and a warm cloak were

not welcome, whilst equally rare were the frost and
snow without a touch of which the return of winter
seems a doubtful thing. Where neither trees nor
hedges are, "vernal bloom" can only exist in the
imagination; and, as for "summer roses," they were
as rare with us as was the sight of the "human face
divine." It may be "pleasant," as the poet writes,
to read

> "Of the great Babel, and not feel the crowd;
>   To hear the roar she sends through all her gates
>   At a safe distance, where the dying sound
>   Falls a soft murmur on the uninjured ear."

Pleasant—yes, but under certain reservations, as
I think the gentle poet would himself have been
ready to admit; nor is there any existing thing so
good but that you *may* chance to have too much of
it. A "murmur" may be so soft that it fails to
make itself heard at all; and when from "the cheerful ways of men," an exile feels that he is destined
to be for life "cut off," the "boding brain" will sometimes reel under the prospect which such a future
unfolds. "The mind is its own place," so said the
master spirit; and this axiom, being classical, must
not of course be disputed; but, on the other hand,
it must be remembered that the "body" has also

its " own place," the which may sometimes seriously interfere with the mind's power of choice and action.

The consequences of being debarred from companionship and converse with one's kind grow in time to be very deleterious : good is it sometimes to listen to other voices than our own ; good to hear talk of new and pleasant books, which are as " living tongues "

" Speaking from printed leaves ; "

good to have our opinions—opinions which have, mayhap, grown rusty as we ourselves have become dogmatic and self-concentrated—traversed, and it may be, wholesomely shaken by converse with those who have been living a larger life, and have seen the things thereof through the right end of the telescope. Of " good " such as this we, alas ! were deprived, *but* happy perhaps was it for some of those whom fate had led into the Wild West that the need of human companionship was one which they felt not. Constant out-of-door exercise, the management and responsibility of a " great concern," the heavy expenses and anxiety attendant on which frequently leave farmers, not only little money to " lay by," but still less leisure for intellectual occupations,—all these things taken together are advantages which an exiled woman, especially if accident has deprived her of the means of out-of-door locomotion, possesses not.

There came a time, however, when circumstances, over which *this* exile fortunately *had* control, enabled her to procure the blessings which healthy occupation alone can give. A garden, and not only a garden, but a conservatory and tiny stove-house, became adjuncts of our dwelling. "The wilderness began (for me) to blossom as a rose," and a school, long the object of my ambition, was set on foot within a mile of the house. The formation of the ground on which I had to work rendered picturesque beauty easy of production, and, climate aiding, it was not long before the Dhulough gardens became a "sight to see." Those who can understand how greatly a "poor thing" is prized if only it is "one's very own," will be able to appreciate the value which I set upon what did in more ways than one proceed from the *coinage* of my brain. It was only just that the expenses of these "enterprises" should not be borne by one who not only had plenty to do with his money, but who did not care, as the country people in the West say, a "ha'p'worth" whether garden flowers

or towering thistles, ragweed or hydrangeas, blossomed
in wild luxuriance within the entrance gates.

To one unaccustomed to the rapid growth on the
Western coast of such trees and shrubs as suit the
climate, the suddenness with which the land, so
lately a half-drained mountain covered with sedge,
blunted heather, and bog myrtle, together with
various weeds innumerable, was transformed into a
blooming garden (one which was in truth worth
travelling many a mile to see) would seem little short
of a miracle. The commoner kinds of evergreens,
such as laurels, laurestinas, Portugal laurels and rhodo-
dendrons, must have made growth at every season
of the year, so rapidly did they shoot up into trees ;
whilst deodaras, Araucarias, Wellingtonias, all the
newer and tenderer kind of firs, were (if they could
but rejoice in a little shelter) but little behind the
hardier kinds in their swift and glorious development.
But, charming as were the evergreen shrubbery walks
which, winding amongst the natural hollows of the
mountain sides, led to trickling streams, which at
flood times were often rather inconveniently full,
the flowering plants (plants that in most parts of
England must be housed in winter, and which, save
perhaps in the Scilly Islands, never even in the more

favoured south attain to any considerable size or
vigour) formed by far the most remarkable feature
of our "grounds." Imagine, dear reader, if you
can, hedges of fuchsias at least ten feet in height;
veronicas usually in full and luxuriant blossom till
December, and nearly rivalling the fuchsia plants in
stature; hydrangeas of so large a size that I have
counted eighty huge blossoms upon one plant,—and
you will be able to form some faint idea of the
wondrous luxuriance of growth, which an habitually
mild and rainy climate is capable in some instances
of producing.

But, *en revanche*, it worked in many ways disastrous mischief. To roses, both climate and soil (aid
the latter as you will) were here terribly unsuited,
while "bedded out" plants, especially heliotropes
and verbenas, could make no head at all against the
soaking rains that descended pitilessly upon their
fragile heads.

Many and various were my efforts at acclimatiza-
tion. It seemed hard to give up the culture of old
favourites known and cherished in days gone by;
but experience and disappointment bore their fruits
in time, and I learned at last the wisdom of not
attempting an unequal contest with Nature. Such

shrubs and plants as after a fair trial refused to adapt themselves to their altered circumstances, I threw aside as earth-cumberers: truly there were enough amongst those which did "flourish like a green bay-tree" (a tree, by the way, which together with the arbutus ranked amongst our most quickly growing evergreens), to make amends for the absence of those, that, like unwilling exiles, pined hopelessly on a soil which was alien to their own.

CHAPTER XXI.

THE CHURCH MISSION REFUSES CONCESSIONS.—JOHN OF TUAM
INSISTS UPON "EMBLEMS," AND MY SCHOOL BECOMES A
FAILURE.—FATHER PAT'S INGRATITUDE.

FOR a time the school, which was situated on the
confines of a wood well known to anglers by the
somewhat eccentric name of "Delphi," struggled
bravely against the obstacles which it had to encounter. With considerable difficulty I secured the
services of a very intelligent and sensible "mission"
schoolmaster, the impediments in my way consisting
chiefly in the obstinate determination of the proselytising authorities to relax no single one of the rules
which they had laid down,—*the* one amongst their
"institutions" which I felt to be in this case of the
greatest importance to break through being that
which made it compulsory on schoolmasters to insist
upon the Bible being read, and the Protestant
faith being *severely* inculcated within the walls of
the school-house.

"But," I argued, "if you do not in this matter (at the Delphi school, at least) give way, not a single Roman Catholic child will be allowed to receive instruction there."

"Better they should stay away," was the bigoted answer, "than that we should exclude the Bible from a school in which the banner of Protestantism should be upheld, and where the Scriptures are recognised as a watchword against the 'idolatrous blasphemies of the Church of Rome.'"

"But," I continued (for I was loth to give up the point, and it seemed so hard that the narrow-mindedness of a few violent party-spirits should stand in the way of at least thirty children receiving the advantages of education—advantages which their parents, one and all, were so anxious to obtain for them), "does it not strike you as possible that merely to instruct the children—to open their minds to the all-important truth that they are deceived, hood-winked, and kept in a state of unnatural bondage by their priests—would be in itself an immense point gained? We must not expect miracles; and what is done slowly is generally done better than hurried and ill-considered work."

Thus much I urged, but urged in vain. Of a piece with the injudicious, hot-headed performances of the tactless, under-bred young men whom they dispatch on their controversial errands are the tactics of their superiors; and can we wonder that in dealing with a shrewd people, and with those who are especially quick to recognise and respect a *real* gentleman, these "sons of thunder" should have signally and ignominiously failed. They are, as a rule, stupidly unmindful of the expediency of gaining an influence over the *women*, for the fear of being "ballyragged" by their wives would alone, in my opinion, be sufficient (even if no other obstacles existed) to keep the men from the degradation (as they deem it) of becoming "joompers." It is not alone in civilised and educated countries that in the weakness of women lies the chief power of the bitterest tyranny that exists on the earth. It is hardly, methinks, too much to say that if there were no weak women in the world there would possibly be neither powerful Pope, nor Ritualistic parsons—good men, many of them, doubtless, and perhaps not altogether to blame in that they take advantage of the foibles of our sex to obtain their ends; a sin, if it be one, in which I shared when I made capital out of the natural jealousy evinced by the wife of Larry Toole of the superior educational advantages enjoyed by the child of John Kennedy, the Scotchman, to induce her to send *her* offspring also to the Delphi school. But alack for me and for my want of moral courage! For not only had I promised Father C——, the Louisberg priest, that if he would allow the children of his flock to attend the school, he might rely on no religious instruction being given them, but I was coward enough to keep secret from my unbending mission correspondent the promise which I had made! Nor was this all. By the aid of some few *indulgences*, the schoolmaster, being persuaded probably that the end justifies the means, forbore to attack the priests and their religion, contenting himself with causing the Protestant scholars to read daily a portion of the Bible, during which reading those of the Romish faith might, if they chose, leave the school-house.

Well, as I said before, the undertaking to a considerable extent prospered; no complaints were heard, and I hoped—vainly, as it turned out—that this new source to me of interest and occupation, might escape the interference of the "clairgy." The Church of Rome, however, according to my belief, neither slumbers nor sleeps; and the love of power, with which its priesthood is possessed, induces that body to neglect not the smallest object over which it may have a chance to tyrannize. In the case of my poor little school, very stringent measures were, it will be seen, taken by those, to defy whose authority our papistical people did not, for a moment, dare.

On one exceptionally fine day in August, I, being then in the small exotic fernery, which in imagination carried me many a mile from chilly Ireland, was suddenly informed that two open carriages, both as full as they could hold of "travellers," were about to turn "round the rock" on the road that led to Delphi. In a moment, being alone in the house, I brought a field-glass to bear upon the enemy, and discovered that a "cloud," not of "majors," but of priests were darkening the horizon! That they had gone to "inspect" the school did not for a moment enter my head, and yet, *que diable allaient ils faire dans cette galère?*

Possibly, though not probably, those eight black-coated men (for eight I had ascertained there were), had been seized with a desire to see "the moun-tains," and were out on a *schockarawn* accordingly; or they might—seeing that the only burial ground

in this mountain district was in the most dilapidated and disgraceful condition—have taken it
into their reverend heads to inspect the place,
and to make arrangements for the more decent
interment of the bodies of the faithful.

Whether or not to either of these causes could
be attributed the length of time which elapsed before
I again caught sight (at the turn of the very sharp
rocky angle that shuts out any further view of the
public pathway) of the horses' heads matters little.
One fact is certain, namely, that the idea of *my*
receiving a visit from these mysterious gentry never
for a moment occurred to me.   Judge then of my
surprise, when—I having by that time almost given
up thinking about them—a "boy " ran up breath-
lessly from the stables with the information that the
Archbishop of " Tume," and " all the clairgy " were
driving up to the house !   This was indeed a surprise;
and as from the drawing-room window I watched
the descent, in the first place, of a stalwart priest,
and then, resting a hand on his arm, that of a very
old, but still erect and apparently healthy old man,
the wish that it had not fallen upon me (in my unprotected state) to receive this extremely unwelcome party
was very strong within me.   There was, however, no

help for it, and nothing remained but to receive my visitors courteously, and wait for an explanation of the visit.

After shaking hands with "John of Tuam," regarding whom I had of course heard much, and exchanging bows with the remainder of the confraternity, who, as it appeared to me, stood in great awe of their vigorous ruler, the latter took upon himself to explain the reason of his coming so far (he had never, he said, visited this portion of his diocese before) into the mountains.

"We have known for some time past," he said, "that there is a mission school, as it is called, in this neighbourhood; but I delayed, till I could take the journey, doing anything about it. We have been into the school-house now, and made sure of its being true (as I was informed), and that there are no emblems in the place."

"Emblems, your Grace !" I put in (for I addressed him according to his legitimate clerical rank, though he did speak with a brogue, and was not *quite* the cleanest old man with whom I had ever come in contact). "Emblems !" I repeated. "I beg your pardon, but my ignorance in such matters must be my excuse. The room, too, in which your Grace has been is private property, and, although, had you asked for it, I should willingly have given you permission to—"

But I was not allowed to proceed. John of Tuam had clearly not bearded the Pope of Rome on his throne, to be "put down" in her own small drawing-room, by a woman. With a wave of his hand, at which his satellites looked high approval, he proceeded to say that until "emblems" were applied to the walls of the school-house he could not permit it to exist. Emblems were with "the Church" a *sine quâ non*, and emblems the old Archbishop declared that he would have.

Oh! how at the authoritative words the free British blood within me boiled and stirred! By what right, I longed to ask him (only he was so old that I refrained), could he close a school which was built on another man's land, and over which he could claim no *earthly* power? The truth was that, being of an autocratic nature and in the habit of saying that his will—namely, that of "the Church"—was "law," he, in a senile kind of fashion, went a step too far. Close the school he of course could not, but the power was undoubtedly his to prevent any Roman Catholic child from entering it, and this power he clearly intended to exercise. A priest has only to threaten the parents with refusal to, in their last moments, " anoint " them, and, ardently as they desire to have their children rescued from ignorance, not one amongst them would, I venture to say, brave the fearful menace which is, in the hands of the priesthood, a weapon of such tremendous force.

After a short while the old man and I understood each other. I explained to him how carefully I had guarded the children of the Romish Faith from any interference with their religion. "But," I said, " *we* Protestants have also our prejudices, and our points of belief. In the Delphi School there are nearly as many Presbyterian as there are Catholic children, and I greatly doubt whether any one of the Scotch- men would, in the event of your Grace's *request* " (and I laid a marked stress upon the word) " being complied with, allow their little ones to come to school. Strive as I may, I have never been able to make them understand that you Catholics are not worshippers of wood and stone and painted canvas ; and therefore the poor things would see in the emblems of which you make so great a point; simply the idols to which you are accused of addressing your prayers."

It is needless to relate the conversation, one of
no long duration, which ensued. It ended (after my
visitors had been offered refreshment, and had refused to partake of our bread and salt) in my informing the Archbishop that I possessed no power
whatever in the matter of which he had been speaking. I would, I told him, consult "the Captain,"
and also the Protestant parents, as to the advisability
of placing crucifixes, pictures of the Blessed Virgin,
&c., &c., &c., upon the interior walls of the school-
house. Eventually I would, I said, inform him of
the result.

"It was chiefly for the Scotch and English that
the affair was set on foot," I concluded by saying,
"and if they object to their admission, I will not be
the one to force upon their children's notice that
which is repugnant to their own feelings."

"Then I have your promise?" the old man said
unctuously, as he held my hand at parting.

"My promise that I will do my best, without
giving offence to others, to afford to those poor little
ignorant waifs and strays, whose parents are so
earnestly craving for it, the blessings of education.
We cannot in any way coerce in this matter our
Protestant *employés*. The decision is one for their

own consciences alone to make, and we should con-
sider ourselves as guilty of wrong-doing were we to
interfere with them; whilst, on the other hand, we
should undoubtedly be equally blamable if we paid
no respect to the feelings and convictions of the
Catholics who depend for their daily bread upon
our retaining them on the land."

These were amongst the last words which passed
between me and this undoubtedly remarkable man,
—this most pugnacious of the Church Militant's
Western Champions. I had given him a hint—but
only a hint, for, in truth, I felt thoroughly ashamed
of the efforts that had been made by zealous prose-
lyters to induce us to force our papistical people, on
pain of eviction, to attend our churches, and otherwise demean themselves as converts,—I had given the
redoubtable "John of *Tume*," then, a hint that, "an we
would, we could" use engines calculated still farther
to depopulate the country, and possibly, though
not probably, secure to the heretics a "joomper"
or two from their forefathers' faith; but, instead of
being aroused by the mild suggestion, he clearly
considered the semi-threat too puerile to be noticed.
Escorted, as on his arrival, by his *aides*, the old man
went his way, an obstinate resolve to hold his own.

being clearly visible on every line of his strongly-marked countenance.

It is, perhaps, scarcely necessary to say that, after this domiciliary visit, not a single Roman Catholic child ever set its foot again in Delphi School.

I was very sorry, but no remedy for the evil could be found. Had the very mildest token of Papistical authority been permitted inside the school house, I verily believe that our stalwart Ross and Inverness-shire shepherds would have risen, as one man, against the contamination which had taken place. Nay, there was one of them, John Kennedy, of whom I have before spoken, as being as *douce* and quiet a specimen of a Celt as ever trudged on heather, whose mind, already disturbed by the talk of " Church Dis-establishment," with which the brains and tongues of all classes were rife, would, I think, have utterly given way, had the slight innovation of which I have spoken been permitted to exist.

It was about a week after the Archbishop's visit that one of his clergy, the "Father Pat," *alias* Priest C——, of whom mention has already been made, got—"honest man" (as the Scotch say)—"into grief" at Bundoragha. He had been holding, in company with another priest, a "Station" in that interesting village,—a "station" being (as I may, for the information of the uninitiated, state), neither more nor less than an opportunity for the Confession by the peasantry, of their sins.

These recognised occasions for putting money into the priests' pockets, occurred, on an average, three or four times a year, and were always held in the cabin of the "best-to-do" of the flock whose sins the Father was ready, after confession and the due payment of fees, to remit.

The expense attending these Stations was considerable, and fell entirely on the *favoured* individual whom the Fathers honoured with their company. As a matter of course, there was provided for their regalement, a goose, as *pièce de résistance*, and whisky *ad libitum*. Should the weather prove unfavourable for "Father Pat's" return after dark along the dangerous bridle-path to Louisberg, he and his pony were housed for the night in the abode where the Station had been held.

On the occasion to which I refer, the weather had been throughout the day more than usually stormy, and therefore no surprise was felt at the absence on the road of any sounds that were indicative of the return of the two priests, the echo of whose ponies' galloping hoofs could usually be heard from the Lodge as they rattled away beneath the windows.

It was not till the following morning that the absence of the accustomed sounds was accounted for. "Father Pat," (as a "boy" from Bundoragha arrived in hot haste to say), had been taken ill in the night, and was now "lying stretched" at Devanney's (our head boatman's) cabin, and "desthroyed enthirely with a pain insoide of him."

Under these circumstances, and considering the sex and vocation of the sufferer, it was "the Captain," and he only, who could venture to prescribe for the invalid's malady. A sick priest with a bad pain "insoide of him," was clearly beyond *my* personal superintendence, so I contented myself with dispatching some simple remedies, such as chlorodyne, brandy, and calomel to the cabin in which the patient lay. As matters turned out, I might have spared myself the trouble of sending more than one specific out of the five—*id est*, brandy. "A hair of the dog that had bitten him," was all that "Father Pat," who had been "glorious" the night before, required! As he lay writhing with pain on Peter Devanny's bed (the two priests had occupied this uninviting-looking couch conjointly), he faintly implored his visitor

to give him, " in the name of God, a dhrop of the crathur."

It was this same priest who, on a later occasion of a similar kind, paid us a visit at the Lodge, and made a singular return for the hospitality and kindness which he received. The ostensible object of his call was to ask for a contribution for a new church which was about to be built at Louisberg, but after obtaining even a larger cheque than he had ventured to hope for, he said insinuatingly, and whilst casting piteous glances at the window, against the panes of which the wild south-west wind was driving perfect *sheets* of rain—

" Bedad, and it ain't weather for a Christian to be out in, at all. Ye don't happen, whishper now, Captain, to have a spare flask with a dhrop o' sperits in it, to keep the cauld out, for I'm fairly moidhered wid the wetting I got on the road as I came along."

There was no resisting this appeal. The weather certainly was frightful, and Father Pat, although a rather decided inebriate, was an old man, and scarcely possessed bodily strength enough to dare the dangers of such a mountain path as the one which lay before him. Steep, almost, as the side of a house, the rough-hewn, staircase-like path, took, after the manner of

precipitous watercourses, many erratic deviations,
one of which lay for a considerable distance along
the giddy verge of the declivity, beneath which, at
the depth of a hundred feet at least, lay the "black
lake," now raging under the lash of the "chainless
winds" that roared so piteously around its shores.

Very much *à contre cœur* was an invitation to
remain the night given to the Priest, and right glad
were we when (the said invitation having been declined) he—mounting his sure-footed little Connemara
pony—went his way, a soda-bottle full of good whisky
in his pocket, and "lashings" of thanks upon his lips.

Will it be believed that on the Sunday but one
that followed on our Good Samaritan-like deed, this
Louisberg priest fulminated from the altar against
us, and likewise caused to be published in the
local Roman Catholic papers, the most bitter and
the most inciting denunciations to murder? The
"Scotch adventurer" was to be "smashed up;" his
people and he, who were robbers of "the countryman's home," were to be desthroyed enthirely, and
his "flocks and herds" were to be "got rid" of, so
that "God's human creatures might have their rights
again."

We endeavoured to have this threat brought

under parliamentary notice, but there are times when it suits a " Conservative " government to shut its eyes to glaring wrongs, and to abuses that call ever so loudly for redress; and as England was at that crisis passing through one of those disastrous phases, it followed that our " far cry " (a distant one indeed, seeing that it came from the Western extremity of the land) failed to make itself heard. That no notice was, at such a time, taken of a complaint, the like of which was, at that season, frequently urged upon the attention of the Government will perhaps occasion but little surprise.

CHAPTER XXII.

I SCARCELY think it is exaggeration to declare
that during our twenty-two years of exile there was
but one month of really warm summer weather,
weather in which a fire not only could be dispensed
with, but would be, by the generality of womankind,
shunned as an objectionable adjunct; and singular
enough to say, that month, one which is fixed upon
my memory by a tragical event, was the frequently
stormy one of September.

As happened sometimes, but rarely—even in the
shooting season—we had a guest within our gates. He
was not much accustomed to the use of fire-arms, an
unfortunate circumstance, of which we had, however,
no knowledge, when he, mounting in *débonnaire*
fashion the sure-footed Connemara pony that had
been provided for his use, trotted gaily away from
the entrance-door for a day's shooting. A wondrous

P

day for beauty and for brightness was the one which
was destined to end in sorest anxiety and trouble.
Not a breath of wind stirred the waters of the lake.
On its smooth surface, every rock and fern frond,
every clump of heather, and every jutting holly was
reflected with a clearness which caused the actual
line that separated land from water to be well nigh
as imaginary as is that of the equator, when beneath
a " hot and copper sky " men " cross the line."

Quietly and indolently sped by the hours, and it
was late in the afternoon when, to my surprise, I
saw, approaching the house, a " man from the West,"
who, as I was well aware, was in the habit of joining
the shooting parties when their course lay seawards.
There was that in the man's face which betrayed him
as a messenger of evil, and his answer to my question of " Well, Heraghty, what has brought you here?"
confirmed me in the terrified suspicion which I had
formed.

" Ach Musha thin, yer honour, but it's the jintleman as is desthroyed enthirely. The roight hand of
him's shot off, an' he nine miles away on the
mountain beyant. I was tould to give yer honour
the word, and that the Captin has tied up the
waound, and the jintleman will be here on Kelly's

horse baste, by the blessing o' God, in an hour's time whativer."

This was indeed terrible news! and as, on further inquiry, I found that a "boy" on horseback had already been sent to Westport for the parish doctor who "practised" there, I had nothing to do but to wait with what patience I could muster for the arrival of the wounded man. The thought of my own powerlessness in such a case for any useful purpose was very trying. In anticipation of every-day accidents, I had made myself acquainted with the simple remedies which were required in such cases. I could apply a tourniquet; with the mysteries of cupping I was familiar, and even the stitching together of a cut, although not the most pleasant use to which a needle can be put, was one which on occasion I had found to be of very considerable utility; but of the treatment of gun-shot wounds I was, alas! as ignorant as a babe unborn, and, coward that I was, I confess to selfishly dreading the very sight of pain, to assuage which I could do absolutely nothing.

It was *then* that for the first time I felt, in its bitterest acuteness, the evil not only of our immense distance from all medical assistance, but the wrong which was done to us by the absence of that to which I felt we had a right.

On an occasion when I had openly expressed my opinion on this subject to one in authority, the answer was—

"If people choose to settle in 'distant places,' they must take the consequences. What do they do in Australia, where perhaps they are fifty, or even a hundred miles from a town, and from a doctor ? "

What, indeed ? But two blacks do not make a white; and the answer, coming as it did from one who never knew an anxiety or a pain which money could lessen or remove, appeared to me by no means conclusive. As in the case of the Errive Bridge that was carried away, petty disputes, and everlasting L. s. d. differences between local contending interests, caused great individual wrongs; whilst a few timely concessions, dictated by a liberal spirit, might have modified, at least, if not removed some of the evils of which so many endured the cruel consequences.

Our first act, after the return of the sufferer, whose calamity had been by no means exaggerated, was to send off the coachman by hired cars to Galway; thence, he was instructed to telegraph to Dublin for

the prompt attendance of the far-famed surgeon,
Mr. Rynd. All haste did the messenger (an experienced traveller) make for the attainment of the
much desired end ; nevertheless, it was not till the
third morning after the accident that the surgeon,
having left his carriage at the village of Leenane in
County Galway, put in an appearance ; immediately
after which welcome event an agonising operation
(one which no local doctor could have been trusted
to attempt), was successfully performed.

In order to give the reader some idea of the
reasons why the patient, during those weary days
and nights, as well as the anxious watcher by his
bed, was doomed thus long—with the ever-present
dread of lockjaw, mortification, and other horrors
before them—to suffer, I will devote a few lines to
the following of the willing Mercury upon his way.

Amongst those who may do me the honour to
peruse this " ower true " journal, there may be some
to whom far Western Connaught is a *terra incognita ;*
and to these I will volunteer the information that
immediately on crossing the Killery Bay, " Charley
Daly " (a well-known character in the " West ")
found himself in County Galway, and eke in Connemara proper,—Connemara, amongst whose " rolling

hills," live the "big Joyces," and where "Paddy of
the wives" (himself a "Joyce") enjoys with his—
as some affirm—two dozen help-meets, an *otium cum
dignitate* which, it may be supposed, is not without
its charms. Famous "evermore" has been the
patthern, or fair of Leenane for its fierce faction-
fights—fights in which Greek met Greek, or, in
other words, when the Connemara "boys" meeting
those of Mayo, "upped" with their shillelaghs, and
gave, as well as got, under the influence of *doctored*
whisky, more broken heads than (saving at far-famed
Donnybrook) are to be found in all "ould Oirland"
put together.

It was the "tourist's" season, and withal exceptionally fine weather, consequently, the little well-bred
mare which the landlord of the Leenane Inn caused
to be harnessed to "Mister Daly's" cair, had scarcely
—to all appearance at least—a leg to stand upon.

With a critic's eye our emissary scanned the
heaving flanks and trembling knees of the over-
worked animal.

"Ach, Musha thin, it isn't further than the crass
roads that the crathur will be going, anyway. Ach
now, docther," continued he, addressing the landlord, who claimed to have been formerly a medical

practitioner at New York,—"Ach now, docther, you'll shurely be giving me something bether the day, an me afther fetching the docther from Daublin for the gintleman as has left his fingers on the moor."

"Is it for that you're hurrying on," asked the doctor. "Bedad, thin, if it had been a poor man's fingers, he'd a got well enthirely widout throubling the Daublin faculty with his ailments. Niver you fear, though; the mare'ull git you to Ougherard safe enough. A betther ain't in the three counties. Shure hasn't she the dhrop? And didn't one of her blood run in the Curragh stakes afore ever I went to York?"

"And wid that," continued, on his return, the relator of the dialogue, "Pat Murphy ups on the sate, and wid a houray, and a 'git on out o' that,' he flogs on the mare, and 'send ye safe homes' follow the crathur up the hill."

But to those who, fortunately for themselves, have only a limited acquaintance with the difficulties attendant on Irish outside-car posting, it will be no news to say that the convulsive canter into which Pat Murphy had urged his steed very soon subsided into a walk; and that eventually more than eight hours were expended in covering the distance of thirty Irish miles which lay between Leenane and the then nearest telegram station.

On the messenger's arrival at Galway, the magic hour of twelve had struck ; and, although informed that it was a case of life or death, nothing could induce the official in charge to work—after hours—the telegraph machinery. The next day being Sunday caused still farther delay ; and thus it happened that not till six o'clock on Monday morning did our messenger bring to us in safety the help that we had so eagerly watched and waited for.

And here I must pause a moment to remark that not only were miles upon miles on the *Mayo* side of the Killery Bay in an utterly destitute condition (as regarded medical aid), but that the same deplorable condition of things existed over a large tract of country, from which only the bay divided us. For many years, in fact until quite recently, no philanthropic desire to lessen the sum of human misery caused such a junction between the parochial authorities of the two counties as resulted in a medical officer living in Galway being available for the necessities of the neighbouring county. After all, however, the boon, when granted, proved to us useless.

Better *no* doctor than either a *cheap* one, or a man who, from moral cowardice, or the evil habit of "drink," renders valueless the good gifts which Nature and education may have bestowed upon him.

After the operation, the surgeon at once proclaimed his intention of taking his patient back with him to Dublin,—a decision which, as was only natural, sounded as the voice of doom to the ear of the maimed and enfeebled sufferer. Death seemed to him, poor man, at that moment, so near, that the Reaper's cold, hard fingers were as though already clutching at his heart.

"I will make it well worth his while to stay here with me. Ten thousand pounds, tell him,"—so spoke the patient in his nervous agony to me—"shall be his, if he will consent to what I ask. If I go to Dublin now, I shall die—I know I shall—upon the road."

This proposition, when I, the intermediary, made it to Mr. Rynd, was received with a simple astonishment that was characteristic of the man. That he— he to whom so many looked for comfort, succour, *life*—could, for anything this world might offer, desert his Dublin patients, was evidently an idea too preposterous to be even for a moment entertained.

"Nonsense," said the *medico*, whose sporting, as well as kindly and generous instincts induced him invariably to refuse the fees of men whom accidents in the hunting-field had caused to need his aid. "Nonsense; tell him, from me, I *can't* remain, and that he must be for some weeks within call of a more experienced practitioner than there is to be found, I reckon, in these parts. Make his servant get him ready; I will answer for it, he won't die."

"To bear is to conquer our Fate!" a truth which, as we carried him off with us to Dublin, our frightened guest probably recognised, for he made no further protest, sitting, in the brightness of the early morning, very white and silent, as the boatman rowed swiftly up the Bay.

Methinks that I shall not, while memory holds her seat, forget the glorious beauty of the scene that then lay stretched out before us. To the one amongst us who felt himself already to be within the jaws of Death, Nature's voice was mute; not so, however, was it to the man of Cities, by whose fiat our poor guest was, according to his own belief, about to be given over to the Destroyer.

"Never in my life have I witnessed any sight so beautiful. Truly, to live in such a paradise of loveliness would compensate a man for being debarred henceforth from sharing in the excitements of City life, and from the pleasure of listening to the busy hum of men,—hum they never so charmingly."

So spoke as he gazed (the boat gliding smoothly onward) the high-hearted surgeon, who, it having been his fate to dwell in streets and squares, had never dreamed till now that Nature in his native land could display such a scene as this. And truly, as I have said, the prospect was one capable of awakening enthusiasm even in the coldest breast. Beneath the bright rays of the morning sun, the Bay, majestically broad, slept like a resting giant. Piled close and high, and "tinged with a lustre proud," the steeps sloped down towards the water's brink. On Muilhrea's mountain—highest of the range—fell the soft lustrous rays,

> "And as each heathy top they kissed,
> It gleamed—a purple amethyst."

I did not attempt to lessen the charm of the present by any description of the reality, which, as regards the paradisial qualities of the Western Highlands, too certainly exists. Never, probably, by the man whose eyes were now raised so admiringly to those mountain heights, would be heard the desolate monotone that for many days and weeks together sweeps in "stormy sobs" over that wild, depopulated region. On *his* memory the scene would ever rest as one of exquisite and fairy loveliness, and therefore I kindly concealed from him the reverse of the medal. Not a word did I say to him of the pithy question dryly put one day to me by a friend "Well, is that shower over yet?"—the "shower" thus waggishly alluded to being a fortnight's downfall of rain, to which the unhappy man had been exposed during a fortnight's tour in Connemara! Equally reticent was I regarding another trifling anecdote connected with the peculiarities of the Connaught climate. Two elderly ladies, hailing from a less pluvious locality than the above, were, at a certain Dublin exhibition, standing in mute wonder before Danby's famous picture of the Deluge. Being but simple folk, the subject thereof failed to make itself clear to their understandings; but upon a by-stander quietly informing them that the delineation was neither more nor less than that of a "summer's shower in the West of Ireland," the visitors from drier lands went their ways, well satisfied with the solution of the mystery.

It may, perhaps, be thought that I have dwelt too long on an incident to which only private and individual interest can be attached; but I have done so chiefly for the reason of impressing upon the minds of those, who live at even a moderate distance from medical aid, the advantage of one individual, at least, in a household, being able to employ, in cases of emergency, remedies which, to be effectual, must be *immediately* applied. I find it hard to understand how any woman can, from *choice*, make herself acquainted with things appertaining to doctor's work, nevertheless such knowledge may prove, on occasion, "most excellent." For instance, had I not chanced to know the symptoms of coming "mortification" occasioned by over-tight ligature, my patient—so said Mr. Rynd—would probably have been a dead man long before *his* arrival at Dhulough. Enough, however, for the present on this theme, but I cannot close this chapter without one more reference to that loveliest morning, when

> "Apollo's upward fire
> Made every Eastern cloud a silvery pyre
> Of brightness so unsullied, that therein
> A melancholy spirit well might win
> Oblivion."

Ah! how little, while my eyes rested admiringly

upon those glorious "things of beauty," did the heart within me guess, that ere another soft September sun would tip with brightness those dark craggy heights, the sun of our home would be for ever darkened, and

> " The brightness of their smiles be gone
> From upland, glade and glen."

"There fell upon the house a sudden gloom," and, till the darkness gathered—till the bolt fell (in heavy punishment, might not my conscience whisper, for years of discontent, and sore repining?) I hardly realised what to us *he* had been, whose chair was empty now! Years—long and sorrowful ones—have rolled away since the Reaper came, and took, ah! so suddenly, and in such *seeming* cruelty—our one bright flower away! Time, the slow but merciful healer, has not failed in his accustomed mission; but, as one, who methinks must also have known deep sorrow, has in some page of wisdom beautifully said,—" Our dead are never dead to us till they are forgotten; " and so it comes about, that, as the shadows of Life's evening crowd and thicken, and I sit in my home alone,

> " When the room grows slowly dim,
> And Life's last oil is nearly spent,
> One gush of light these eyes will brim,
> Only to think *he* came and went."

CHAPTER XXIII.

"IF the Irish Church Act passes it will become
impossible for any Saxons to live in Ireland."

Such was the prophecy enunciated to me by one
who knew the West of Ireland thoroughly, and who
dreaded, as did all those equally well informed upon
the subject, the passing of a measure, such as the
one which soon after became law—I speak of the
disestablishment of the Irish Church. That immense and fundamental reforms were necessary in
that Church, there could be no doubt; but, without
entering at all into either the political or clerical
merits of the question, it is sufficient to say that the
Act was passed at a time when it *appeared* to the
Roman Catholic hierarchy that fear of *them* and of
what *they* might, in the way of mischief, be able to
effect, lay at the bottom of the movement. No concessions, by whomsoever made, to popular clamour

have ever been productive of good effects in Ireland. Neither, moreover, to genuine philanthropy, nor to a pure and exalted sense of justice, did the Irish priesthood attribute the act of so-called "justice to Oirland," of which political expediency was, it is to be feared, the *primum mobile.* Indeed, to discover anyone more profoundly ignorant of the real merits of the question than was the originator of the Bill, would have been, I imagine, a difficult task.

Never in his life had Mr. Gladstone set foot in the country which was about, by his agency, to pass through a phase, as momentous, as it was more than suspected to be dangerous. He might, had he chosen, have easily made himself better acquainted with the state of feeling, and of "things" which really existed in the sister island. But he did not so choose. The testimony of the public press, indicative of the highly-wrought pitch of excitement to which "contending parties" had arrived in those parts of the country where a chronic though smouldering state of "disturbance" existed, seems to have been disregarded by him. Freedom— a watchword, which till within these last few sadly eventful years, has ever found an echo in the hearts of the English people, was the one with which "their eyes were darkened that they could not see, and their ears deafened that they could not hear "—Freedom!—whilst in reality he was rendering triumphant, and placing power in the hands of, the most grinding and oppressive tyranny that the world, in the nineteenth century, owns! The "people" themselves in Roman Catholic Ireland, never felt the existence of the Protestant State Church, in their country, as a grievance, till they were hounded on to the fray by the priests, and eventually, by that pugnacious, ever restless body, were taught to believe that England found it necessary for her own safety, to conciliate and grant benefits to Ireland.

For some time previous to the passing of the Act, Ribandism had, with its attendant horrors, been increasing in the country. To those (and they are in an immense majority) who have never chanced to read the "Riband oath"—one which the members of this fearful secret society seek to impose upon all who come within their power—the terrors of its exactions, and the awful nature of its threats would scarcely be believed possible. They take oath (being driven so to do by every species of moral and physical torture which the fiends in human shape

q

who coerce them are able to inflict) that they will
—should the lot to do so fall to them—shoot, kill
and destroy, any and every one whose death is
decreed by the Society. The penalty of refusal is
certain death to themselves, a penalty which, as the
authentic papers I had access to went on to say,
the recusants will find it impossible to escape, even
though they should betake themselves to the utter-
most ends of the earth in search of safety. The
barbarous acts committed by Ribandmen in order
to compel others to take the oath are, some of
them, almost too shocking to be believed. There
is an instrument composed of many teeth, which is
used in the West for what is called "tazing," *anglice*,
teasing the wool, and with this same instrument of
torture the Ribandmen have been not unfrequently
known at dead of night to enter the lonely cabin of
a peasant, and then and there scrape off his skin,
till such time as, in the extremity of his agony,
he enrolled himself as one of the dreaded band of
ruffians.

The priests are mortal enemies to *this*, as indeed
they are to all secret societies—save their own.
With regard to Fenianism it has always been doubtful
to what extent (or indeed, whether at all) they

encouraged its spread. One thing however is certain, that with the acts of lawlessness—acts to which the " clergy " undoubtedly lent their aid and authority, —which promptly followed on the passing of Gladstone's Church Bill, Fenianism made simultaneous, and gigantic strides.

One event, not only of importance to our private interests, but which was the cause, humanly speaking, of an occurrence that throughout the length and breadth of the land sent a thrill of horror and dismay, I have hitherto omitted to mention, and that event was the departure from our service of our valued bailiff, James Hunter. At the end of four years, during which he gave us the great benefit of his skill and experience, he took—as he had always intended eventually to do—a long lease of a farm of considerable extent on the other side of Newport, and on the road to Ballina. His landlord was an Irish Protestant parson, and the rent paid by Hunter for land, the greater part of which cousisted of bog and mountain, was generally said to be higher than the " take " was worth. Still, as was generally allowed to be the case, if any one *could* make the farm of Tierna " pay," that man would be James Hunter. For, independently of his great experience he possessed an iron will, indomitable perseverance, and a rectitude of principle which gained him universal confidence and respect. The cotters, who were small tenants on that part of the Reverend T. G——'s property which surrounded Hunter's farm, were essentially what is called "a bad lot." Lawless, predatory specimens of the human race were they; men, women and children, whose civilisation had never even been attempted. More dangerous neighbours were they by far than the warlike Zulus, inasmuch as the "strong back," on which they leant, was that of a body of human beings professing Christianity, and arrogating to themselves the right to remit sins.

An utterly fearless man was Hunter, and one who never hesitated to perform an act of justice, even though his own feelings might be pained by the deed which he had been called upon to do. As an instance of this, I must mention the shooting, by his own hand, of his beautiful young Collie dog—the identical "Turk" of whom honourable mention has already been made. This act of retribution, which followed quickly on the killing and eating by our canine favourite of one of the "Captain's" lambs, caused universal regret.

"Oh, Hunter!" was my exclamation, when I had heard what had happened, " how could you do it ? You might have punished him, poor fellow— given him away—done anything rather than shoot him ! "

" Punishment would have been just useless," was the grave reply. " Once a dog has tasted a laumb, he's never cured, and to give him awa wouldn't have been right whatever."

Well, to our great regret, James Hunter left us, and took up his abode, with his wife (a quiet, excellent woman) and their two children, at an old house by the sea-shore, which in its lonely ugliness exceeded to my thinking all that I had as yet witnessed of the kind in Ireland. A few miles beyond the town of Newport you come upon a tract of country which may in very truth be called a " howling wilderness." No longer do the beauties of Clew Bay, with its hundred islets, and its rocky, cloud-capped boundaries, meet the eye, but, instead, a dead level of *peat* land, sprinkled with a scanty growth of heather, and with here and there (in spots where discoloured water has filled up the *pits* out of which turf has been cut for burning) tufts of cotton-grass, interspersed with yellow asphodels and bog beans. Low stone

walls, *dry* built, and equally low turf fences,
mark the boundaries of individual holdings ; a few
wretched-looking Irish sheep, often tied together in
pairs to prevent their straying, pick a scanty living
on the miserable soil ; whilst from the wretched
cabins rush unkempt, rag-clad children, who stare
with a look of stupid wondèrment at the few strangers
who pass by their doors.

Those who desire to reach the sea, and, it may
be, pay a visit to the stalwart East Lothian farmer
whose evil genius had cast him upon the bogs of
Tierna, must leave the high road which leads
from Newport to Ballina, and travel for about a
mile and a half along a *cross*, and ill-kept route,
that is bordered on either side by dykes, and by
just such a desert scene as I have attempted to
describe. But previous to relating the occurrence
which, to this day, lends so tragical an interest to
this dreariest of imaginable localities, it behoves
me to sketch with as much brevity as is consistent
with clearness, some of the circumstances which
led, as well directly as indirectly, to the commission
of as foul a crime as ever disgraced this priest-ridden
land.

As I have already said, Jam̲̅ r was both a

courageous and a just person. To ignore the rights of a poor man, let those rights be ever so hazily defined, would have been a dereliction from right principle of which he was totally incapable. Equally at variance also was it with the man's character to abate one jot or tittle of claims which he felt were, upon his own account, founded in strictest justice. Such claims, as well as the "rights" which his lease gave him over the property that he rented, he would, and did, maintain against all comers, trespassers included, (and "trespassers" in the far West are dangerous customers to meddle with,) who ventured to interfere with, and to molest him.

The right of "turbary"—namely, that of cutting turf upon the land, has always been a source of vexed questioning in Ireland. Very lawless are the ways and customs of the half-savages who, on the far side of Newport, people the bog; and away thence to the still wilder regions of Achill, and thereabouts, live men who have long rendered themselves famous for their law-defying qualities; the ways and customs of these wild sons and daughters of Erin being of a kind to render their ideas regarding the rights of property somewhat loose and indistinct. At "their own sweet will" the tied-together sheep,

the lean cow, and the hardy goats of the cotter
tenant had, probably, without let or hindrance,
hitherto browsed; and had so far prospered, that,
by dint of feeding his flocks upon a better-to-do
neighbour's land, the cotter was the more able to
pay, to the exacting parish priest, the dole which
the latter claimed. The advent, under these circumstances, of a tenant such as James Hunter,
upon the scene, was one which both by priest and
peasant was viewed with sovereign disgust, and it
was not long before hostilities of a very suggestive
character were commenced by the aborigines against
the intruder. As we had ourselves, under somewhat
analogous conditions, passed with comparative safety
through similar ordeals, we were not without hope,
seeing that the " times " were not especially " risky,"
that the man who was so pluckily following our
example might eventually weather the storm, and
come out of the strife a winner. A winner, even
as *we* appeared to be, for in the June of the year
of which I am about to write, 23,000 sheep marked
with " the Captain's " brand were grazing on the
mountains, whilst of kine he possessed more than
the *im*patient Job could,—the second time,—boast
of owning !

But meanwhile, a cloud, and that a heavy one, was gathering above the horizon. Everywhere, that is, everywhere in Roman Catholic Ireland, an ill spirit, one which was in a great measure evoked by the passing of Gladstone's Act, began to openly manifest itself. Fenianism was making giant strides, whilst such papers as the " Nation " and the " Flag of Ireland," were openly advocating rebellion, and the expediency of throwing off the hated Saxon yoke. It was about this period that the cowardly crime of sending anonymous threatening letters to those (ourselves included,) who were written of by the Press as " robbers of the poor," and " despoilers of the widow and the fatherless," became alarmingly frequent, after an interval of comparative calm. At this time, tco, Hunter, who had long suffered annoyance from the trespassing across his cropped fields of country carts on their way to gather up the " saved " turf which awaited housing on the cotter's portion of the bog, took out, at length, (his patience being exhausted,) a summons against the chief offender. The case, which was tried at the Newport Petty Sessions, was given against the trespasser (a peasant, whose name was McN——l), and a fine of, I forget what amount, was imposed upon the offender.

This, although he was known to be a "snug man," he neglected to pay, and Hunter, who, though liberal to the poor, was, as I have said, one who held stoutly to his dues, threatened (it was a rash act, but thoroughly characteristic of the determined Lowland Scotchman), to "distrain."

Poor fellow! Little dreamt he that in uttering that word he signed his own death-warrant. It was his habit on Sunday afternoons to drive his wife and children to church at Newport in his dog-cart. This he had done one fine August afternoon, the only difference in the normal order of things being that little Maggie, who had a cold, remained at home, whilst Jamie—at that time an intelligent boy of some ten years old—was, on the family's return to the old house by the sea, seated behind his parents on the dog-cart.

A quiet, yet far from an uncheerful little party. Presbyterians though they were, the Hunters never strove to make Sunday a day of wearisomeness and gloom, and the father had just turned back to his boy a kindly semi-serious face, whilst on his lips a playful remark was lingering, when —Oh, horror indescribable! there broke upon the air a sound—a cry—a fall, and, springing over one of the low **turf** walls which I have before described, there was seen—plainly visible against the summer sky—the figure of a human being.

He had fallen—that big, stalwart man,—shot through the heart—across his wife's knees; and on them, with the poor little frightened boy leading the quiet horse, she (full sure, unhappy soul, that he was dead), for a long, weary mile of way, held him with loving hands, whilst, from eyes in which horror had frozen up their source, tears strove in vain to fall.

It is as needless to dwell upon, as it is impossible to describe, such scenes of grief as this. The widow's only comfort—but it was no slight one—lay in the thought that her husband's death had been a painless one, and the hope, after the first shock was over, of a speedy removal to her own country, and to her father's house, further tended to reconcile her to existence; but in this hope she was destined, as will be speedily seen, to disappointment.

CHAPTER XXIV.

A YEAR OF PERIL.—THE COUNTRY IN ALARM, AND FENIANISM
RAMPANT.

As a matter of course, an Inquest was held on the
remains of the man who had been thus, in the face
of day, foully done to death; and almost equally, as
a matter of course, no result—as regarded the com-
mittal of the offender—followed on the enquiry.
That the murderer was none other than McN——l, the
individual who had been threatened with "distraint,"
and whose long-standing enmity towards the farmer
had for some time been matter of notoriety, no one
entertained a doubt. He was known to have been
in possession of a gun; the widow, and also her son,
were convinced, although they declined to swear to
his identity, that the man whom they saw jump over
the hedge was none other than McN——l. There
was also a servant-girl of Mrs. Hunter's, one Biddy
Moran, whose evidence, given in fear and trembling,
went greatly against the accused; but all this evidence

was unavailing to convict.   The persons who were on the Coroner's Jury either had received, or were afraid of receiving, threats to the effect that if a verdict of "Wilful Murder" against the prisoner—for such McN——l was—were returned, they would soon be all dead men, and so the investigation ended—as such investigations generally do in that miserably ill-governed country—in failure.   "Some Person or Persons unknown" had with remorseless cruelty hurried to an untimely grave the husband and father, whose mortal remains those cowardly, for-sworn men had calmly gazed upon.   So much and no more, had they been willing to admit, and a Verdict to that effect was duly recorded.

Less than a week afterwards, Biddy Moran, fleeing for dear life across the bogs, took refuge one stormy night in the house of our Scotchman, John Shaw. Eighteen miles had the terrified girl run, those who sought her life (Paddy McN——l's *frinds*), tracking her footsteps closely by the way.   But she eluded them, and a few days later we contrived to get her off safely to America, in which country she had relations well-to-do and willing to assist her.

Poor Mrs. Hunter was not so fortunate, being con-demned by adverse circumstances, and sorely against her will, to remain in a country and on a spot which had become hateful to her. Hunter's lease was a long one, and the landlord, a Protestant parson, as I before said, demanded of the widow so heavy a price for the cancelling of the engagement, that the poor woman was utterly unable to pay it. So in that to her naturally most distasteful locality, and farming the land as best she (with the aid of a kindly Scotch neighbour,) could, she with her two children remained ; and there, with the sight of her husband's murderer ever before her eyes, stern necessity holds her still.

This melancholy event happened in the summer of 1869, and the Government—a law having shortly before been passed empowering them so to act—sent a body of Royal Irish Police to the scene of the murder, there to remain, (an iron house having been erected for their reception) till such time as the assassin should be given up to justice. The expense of paying and maintaining the police in their new quarters was, meanwhile, to fall upon the *townland* in which the crime had been committed.

Seeing that by this method of proceeding the innocent suffered for the guilty, it might be supposed by those who are ignorant of the power of "hanging together," (especially as regards the concealment of crime,) for which the Irish are remarkable, that but a short time would probably elapse before the criminal would be denounced by "the neighbours," and the burden of supporting the police be removed from the townland. Far otherwise was, and indeed for that matter, is still the case. Many a year— dragging in storm and tempest its slow length along—has sped by, and as yet the "giving up" to justice of poor, brave Hunter's murderer is as far as ever from being a *fait accompli.*

More than once, as we, to use a West country phrase, "could hear," there had been "divisions in the camp," the innocent declaring with a loud voice that they would no longer suffer for the guilty; but when these dissensions reached the "clairgy's" ears, they invariably put a "stopper" on the impending movement.

"Now, boys, I'll have no quarrelling" was the sum and substance of the parish priest's after-chapel discourse to his obedient flock; and well did the latter both comprehend and obey the orders thus cabalistically given. To threaten, in cases of contumacy, those poor ignorant "dumb dogs," would have been a v   erogation. Disobedience to the Priest's commands is too well recognised as a mortal sin (one to be followed by refusal to "anoint," and by sundry other future pains and penalties terrible in proportion to their vagueness), for the tyrannised-over congregation to even dream of offering resistance. Father Mick, a butcher's son may be, and probably as good a judge of a horse as was to be found " between this and Daublin," had commanded his flock to put a bridle on their lips, and therefore, without comment or resistance, the people remained mute as before, on the subject of the murder.

There began from that time what may be called a reign of terror in Mayo. Invasion on the part of the mysterious Fenians was greatly feared by the Government as well as by unprotected individuals. Beyond, or rather irrespective of Nature's own defences, namely, the dangerous character of the coast, and the frequent tempests (truly effective Armstrong guns, as they burst thunderingly over the storm-tossed waves), there was literally nothing from Galway Bay to Sligo to prevent a landing of the enemy. In consequence of this acknowledged peril—two gunboats—the "Flirt" and the "Orwell" were dispatched for West of Ireland Coast Service, their head-quarters being the Killery B-the County Mayo was "proclaimed," and a body of Royal Irish Police was ordered for our individual protection to Delphi, the small fishing lodge, situated, as I have before said, at half a mile's distance from our house. Nor were these the only precautionary measures which the Government deemed it necessary to take. A spirit of disaffection having begun to show itself amongst the Irish soldiers quartered in the Emerald Isle, no time was lost in removing to other quarters such regiments as were blessed with a preponderance in their ranks of the Celtic element. Such seditious newspapers as "The Flag of Ireland" and the "Nation," were as far as possible repressed, and the small remnant of obnoxious persons, who, during that exciting period, elected to remain in the country, looked well to the condition of their revolvers, and to the ammunition which self-defence rendered it prudent to lay in.

The winter of 1870 commenced, not only for the country generally, but for us individually, under very trying circumstances. Our Ross-shire shepherd, whose district lay in the neighbourhood of Shafry mountain, and whose isolated house stood beneath its giant shadow, unprotected by aught save a few stunted trees, was one nir   · a party of fourteen

men, armed with guns, and with faces closely masked.
Five shots were fired through a window,—that of the
room in which three of Macdonald's children were
sleeping. As had been the case with the attack on
John Shaw's house, the bairns, as if by a miracle,
escaped, the balls passing slantways over the bed,
with an interval of only a few inches between their
small bodies and the line of fire, into the further
wall. The wretches, whose object was probably
intimidation rather than murder, then dragged the
terrified inhabitants of the cottage upon the road
outside, and forced them, on pain of speedy death, to
pledge themselves to leave the country. Nor was
this all, for far worse, in my opinion, remains to tell.
The assailants, hereditary and determined trespassers and sheepstealers, occupied land just over the
"meering," that is, the boundary of our farm, and it
had been a portion of Macdonald's duty, one which
he had most conscientiously performed, to drive, off
(his good collie dog assisting in the work) all sheep
found straying, and of course "supporting" themselves upon the mountains rented by his employer.
Now, to his master, a perfectly trained sheep-dog is
not only the most faithful of friends, but a possession
without which the former cannot, with any degree of

efficacy, carry on the business of his calling. Well aware were these cowardly and cruel nightly visitors that, without the aid of " Bran," the detested Scotchman would have been comparatively powerless to injure them, and, therefore, to avenge themselves upon the innocent instrument of mischief was a preconceived determination on their part, which only too soon became evident. Bran was condemned to die! But not quickly—not by the pulling of a trigger would the wise, gentle animal, whom the whole humble household loved, be hurried out of the world. Bran was to die in torture, torture to the description of which I would not—*could* not listen, but the spectacle of which Macdonald and his family were compelled to witness!

In this case, as in every other, all attempts to procure direct evidence against the perpetrators of the outrage proved vain, and therefore, within half a mile of Macdonald's house, and on a spot as barren and desolate as is possible for the imagination to conceive, another iron house was set up, and another body of the Royal Irish Police was despatched from head-quarters to the "rescue." To "the rescue," so to speak, but still more to act both as a punishment, and as a possible means of throwing light (as regarded the actual guilty ones) upon the case. But, as might have been expected, the attempt proved, also in this instance, abortive. Month after month, and year after year sped by, and still—for the Drummin Priest had put his finger on their lips—the "neighbours," though sorely grudging the payment of their exacted dole, kept silence from any words, good, bad, or indifferent, that might relieve them of their hated burden.

That never-to-be-forgotten winter, a winter which scared away more than one Irish landlord, who might, but for " the state of the country," have done much to benefit its people—that never-to-be-forgotten year, we, contrary to a custom long since established, passed the entire winter in the " proscribed " and dreaded West. Not, as heretofore, did we, after the month of January had set in, depart for a two months' "change" abroad; for a sense of duty detained us; a sense similar in some sort, methinks, to that which bound another conscientious and threatened tenant—(*landlords* in Mayo did not strike me ever in the light of men marked out for slaughter) —to the post of danger. The Scotchmen, 'ten in number, who were in our service, had been, and were constantly and alarmingly menaced, and it was not for those, through whose instrumentality they had migrated so far from home and safety, to desert them in the hour of peril ; and so, each man being duly armed with his revolver, the Presbyterian shepherds pursued, without any sign of alarm or shirking, their accustomed duties, whilst we—— Well, the days and nights went by—our weapons were ever, either in our hands, or on the dining table, on our beds or on the "car" cushions ; and yet, so true a saying is it that "use doth breed a habit in a man," I grew ere long so accustomed to live in daily peril that I sometimes almost forgot to remember its existence. As for my own especial "six-chambered" weapon, I very soon began to look upon it as a vain and futile encumbrance. I had duly learned to use it, and had indeed arrived, whilst shooting at a mark, at some degree of proficiency in the art of self-defence, but—a melancholy fact, and one which I did not attempt to conceal from myself—to shoot straight—nay, even (were my target a human being) to take aim at a living creature would be to me an impossibility. More than one secret notice had I that danger lurked for us behind the thick high laurel hedges which adorned the shrubberies. Certainly there were many places of concealment in the neighbourhood of the lodge where an assassin could lie *perdu,* unsuspected by all or any of us. One notification, written on the coarsest possible paper, and directed to "Lady Houstoun, Esquire," contained a promise from "Rory of the Hills," that if I would "lave the counthry enthirely, no harrum in life would happen" me. True to the letter, I have no doubt; but then how *could* I for a moment contemplate the possibility of following my unknown correspondent's advice? Deep within my breast there lay an unspoken suspicion—one which was afterwards, in a most unquestionable manner, confirmed —that on the fact of my remaining at my post depended possibly the safety of one whose life was of so infinitely greater value than my own. But, be this as it may, of one thing I was at that time, and am still, thoroughly convinced—namely, that if it be the intention, the fixed purpose of those who regulate the proceedings of Irish assassins to have the life of their enemy, *none* of the simple precautions usually taken—such as bearing firearms, &c., &c., &c.—can prevent the carrying out of their fell and cowardly purpose. The shot that is meant to kill is apt to do its work effectually and at once, and in a locality where, as in our case, there is *cover*

in which more than one assailant may lie hidden,
the intended victim has but a slender chance of
escaping with his life. The circumstance that a
notorious " bad subject," a man whose name—
Timony—has been more than once mentioned by
me, and who had three years previously been discharged from our service in disgrace, had returned,
a noted Fenian, from a temporary sojourn in
America, and was hanging, *incog.*, about his old
haunts, was generally supposed to add considerably
to the dangers we were incurring. I, however, did
not fear him. The fellow was a lawless, reckless
scamp—but remembering, as I could not but do, a
certain night, when he (in the isolated cabin at
the far end of Dhulough, where he and his " long,
wake family " abided) hung sobbing—the big strong
man—over what he feared was the death-bed of his
little girl, I felt no fear that he would do aught to
injure either me or mine.

" Had it not been for *us*," said, about this time to
me, a coarse-minded Roman Catholic curate, " the
Captain would have been shot years ago."

A somewhat suggestive assertion this, and one, the
truth of which I see no reason to doubt ; but, even
whilst believing that the boast was not an empty

one, my conviction remained unshaken, that, but for the strong domestic affections of the people with whom we had to deal, our career in the West would certainly have been cut shorter. Attentions— ending perhaps in the saving of life—paid to the children, for whose sake (I speak chiefly of the girls) mothers from their birth begin to lay by a future portion, could hardly fail to excite, in the minds of the Western Irish, feelings with which murder and cruelty had little to do. Kindly-spoken words, too, and a sympathy which they are quick enough to understand is *real*, are far from being thrown away upon a race, in whose veins there certainly runs not "snow broth." That gratitude is with them no lasting feeling, and that "a lively sense of favours to come" is absolutely necessary for its continuance, I had, when my power to benefit them was over, melancholy and ample proofs.

But what mattered it? The "bite" of "benefits forgot" was to me no strange and unaccustomed thing, no novel and startling phase of mental suffering, whilst for the wound there existed a healing balsam, and for the bane an antidote. Not altogether for *nothing* had I, for nearly a quarter of a century, been severed well-nigh entirely from

the society, the sympathy, and (I was almost about
to say) the companionship of my kind. Albeit I
could not flatter myself that in the hearts of even
one of those, whom I had striven to aid, my
memory would greenly live, yet the belief that I
had served a purpose, and been to others a source
of safety, and a means towards a purposed end,

" Softened the heart like sweet music to hear."

More than once have I been asked by friends who
lived at home at ease, whether I did not in those
eventful days often endure personal fear ; and my
answer was always—and that truthfully—in the nega-
tive. The dread, so universally entertained, of sudden
dissolution has always been to me incomprehensible ;
while to be " done to death " by the swift passage of
a bullet through the brain strikes me as a boon
indeed.   Oh ! to be spared the heart-quakings of
anticipation ! The dwelling on material horrors
which *must* come after death—the pain of parting,
not only with friends, but with a world in which
there is so much to interest, so much—so very much
in leaving—to regret ! For such a lessening as this
of the suffering which is entailed on human nature,
are there not some who would be grateful to their God ?

CHAPTER XXV.

THUS passed, in excitement and in turmoil, the winter of 1869—70; and in the spring—happily for Ireland, and for us—Gladstone's strong Coercion Bill checked the gradually increasing number of crimes which his former measure had so greatly aided in producing. Amongst those whose future lot was incidentally, yet materially, decided by that sinister movement, I cannot omit to mention our unfortunate Scotchman, Kennedy. Possibly there was already a taint of madness in the quiet Presbyterian's blood, and perhaps it needed but the poison engendered by religious bigotry and zeal to set the latent evil working. Quietly argumentative at first, he soon grew fierce and wrathful, whilst debating upon the great question which was then stirring up to strife so many throughout all the land. The Queen's name—inasmuch as she had sanctioned the deed which he condemned—"stank," the poor fanatic once said to me, "in his nostrils," nor would he attend our service in the school, for the reason that "She" was there prayed for as "religious." After that act of secession, the poor man's progress towards actual insanity was very rapid—a homicidal mania declared itself, and, to the great sorrow of his wife, he was removed to Castlebar Asylum. By the doctors there he was, after the expiration of two years, pronounced to be incurable, and within those walls he lingers still—a hopeless, but harmless maniac.

Comparative peace (I speak of the peace which is *that* outwardly) succeeded to the "reign of terror" under which so many had groaned; but, although the Government, roused at last to the necessity of doing "something," had applied a salve (and later still—finding that the remedy was no healing one— a *caustic*) to the long-standing and ever-festering wounds they had to deal with—although the Government had done all this, yet not one whit, in reality, was a healthier state of things thereby induced. The priests, though they were, to a certain degree, rendered by the Coercion Act less openly insolent, did not abate one jot or tittle of the "pound of flesh" which they claimed from each

individual of their flock ; still, as before, they were
ever and always "in at the death" of such amongst
the faithful, as were known to have, by strenuous
efforts, and during a long life of toil, saved up a few
precious pounds, the which store did, according to
custom, lie hidden away from "eyes profane" inside,
may be, the dirtiest of mattresses, or the least pre-
sentable of woollen stockings. How great or how
small might be the actual amount of old Mike's or
old Biddy's savings, was in many cases, to their
"frinds" only a matter of conjecture, but the priest,
who alone is "behind the curtain," is better informed. To a shilling does he know the amount of
his penitents' earthly possessions, and long before
the sands of life have fallen so low, that he—the
poor man's spiritual autocrat—has been sent for in
hot haste, the wily "Father" has calculated to what
extent he can, by working upon the sufferer's fears,
cheat the poor relatives out of their due.

Many a time had I heard, and that not from
"heretics" like myself, but from persons of the
priests' own faith (and much by the way did I
marvel that such instances of human frailty in the
keepers of their consciences, did not place the latter
on—in the opinion of their flocks—a lower level),

many a time had I heard related authenticated cases
of the kind just alluded to; but only one such case
came—I feel bound to say—under my own *personal*
observation, and the particulars thereof were as
follows.

Half a mile from our house was situated a thatched
cabin, in which there had lived, for nearly ten years,
an aged woman, blear-eyed and haggard of mien,
who was known by the name of "Granny"—and
indeed by no other. She had never married, but,
alas! in the days of her youth, she had "stooped to
folly," and there was one, a woman of half a century
old (for "Granny" had nearly reached four-score), who
had the right to call our neighbour "mother." Very
poor, and withal weighted with children galore, was
this "daughter of sin," whose husband could earn
but a sorry pittance for his family's support. Never
warmly received by her parent, whose affections
were centred in the children of our cook (she, the
aged crone, having reared them successfully "by
hand"), poor Mary Joyce, whilst aware that "Granny"
had saved money, could hardly have ventured to
hope that *much* of the precious gold would find its
way into her empty pockets. And yet—and yet—on
whom could it be more usefully bestowed, and whose

claim upon her property was so strong as that of the daughter whose inheritance of shame there was no power to cancel now?

More than once did I raise my voice in favour of the often nearly destitute creature, whom "Granny" had cursed with the curse of life.

"You surely will leave your money to Mary Joyce," I said to her. "Think of her many children, and how often she hasn't so much as a potatoe to give them."

"Ach musha, thin, milady, it's but little I have mesel; and me that's to be put underground, and a dacent wake to be paid for wid the few shillings I lave afther me," was the old crone's reply; after making which she would ingeniously turn the conversation to the subject of her own ailments, her weak eyes—all the "wash" for which had been used—and her "bad throat," that sorely needed a fresh supply of paregoric lozenges.

In short, neither I nor the worthy mother of the children she had nursed could make any "hand" of the selfish old creature, whose anxiety regarding the future fate of her immortal soul had entirely closed her heart to the emotions of motherly pity. At length the day came when Father R——, whose

attentions since the grandame's health had declined
had greatly increased, received notice by a swift-
footed messenger that "Granny" lay at the point
of death, and "would his Riv'rence," so said the
boy, "hurry on to see her?"

"Troth, an' I will," answered the priest; and in an
almost incredibly short period of time his horse
could be seen tied to the little wooden gate which
led to the cabin, whilst within—ah! who can say what
"something passing show" did, in that momentous
tête-à-tête, supervene? The result, a fatal one to
the wretched daughter's interests, alone transpired.
"Granny" had died "worth" £15 7s. 6½d., and with
the exception of three pounds, the legacy was made
over—in the person of Priest R——,—to the Church.

Much has been said and sung of the superior
merits (as regards the purity of their morals and
conduct) of Irish girls, and the alleged fact, that
Erin's daughters are as virtuous as her sons are
brave, is almost invariably attributed to the influence of the priests. Now, previous to entering
into the question of how far, if at all, clerical
influence has to do with the matter, I will deal,
as far as my experience goes, with the fact (?)
itself. In the small village of Bundoragha (if

village it can be called, which contained at the
most fifty inhabitants, and a dozen or so of houses
scattered here and there within an area of half-a-
mile) there were to be found—ah, well a day! for
the *girls!*—no less than five illegitimate children,
two of them being the children of sisters, living
under their father's roof. For the existence of these
unfortunates the excuse of overcrowding could not
be urged. The poacher's rebuke to the Squire—a
rebuke, which should be sounded with a ringing cry
in the ears of all those who might, but do not, exert
their influence and devote a portion of their super-
fluous wealth, to the duty of aiding to remove one
of the most fruitful causes of female ruin, would have
struck in our breasts no self-reproaching chord :—
" The rich are mainly answerable for such back-
slidings among the poor." Such was the sum and
substance of the reckless prisoner's rebuke.

A very impertinent one, doubtless ; but although
impertinent, the assertion is none the less true ; and
equally true is it, that for the far too frequent
overcrowding of the cottages in Ireland, the priests
are to a certain extent accountable. Staunch
advocates are they for the early marriages, by
which their "pickings" are increased, and little

does it matter to them that double, and often far more than double the number which a wretched hovel is calculated to hold, are crowded together under its miserable roof. Population, at any cost, is what the " clergy " want, and therefore—to quote for the second time the words of a Saxon Irish landlord for whose absenteeism there is some excuse :— " Paupers are bred to pay priests."

That the boy and girl marriages to which I have alluded may in some cases tend to the hindrance of vice, I am willing to admit; but, as I have just shown, there is a reverse side of the medal, and one which might, if truly reported, tell a different tale. It is not only on occasions when the *Last* Sacrament is to be administered, and the soul of a dying man is to be prepared to meet his God, that the Roman Catholic Hierarchy in Ireland take advantage of a fellow creature's weaknesses in order better to advance the interests of the Church. The equally sacred, though less melancholy rite of marriage is frequently postponed by the parish priest, till such time as the families of the affianced pair can, between them, produce a fee sufficiently large to satisfy the holy Father's cupidity. Love, in the human breast is doubtless a powerful passion, but Fear, coupled with love of

s

money, is, I am afraid, in poor Paddy's nature a mightier motive agent still, for the delays occasioned by clerical rapacity were often of long duration—so long indeed as to sometimes justify a doubt as to the existence in the *Promessi Sposi's* hearts of any purer, stronger passion than the universal one—for filthy lucre.

CHAPTER XXVI.

BEFORE bidding a final adieu to scenes, which not
even the thickest and most sombre of curtains can
ever shut from memory's retrospective eye, the spirit
within me is moved to say a few last words regarding certain especial days and incidents, which (probably because they belonged to the later days of my
sojourn in the country) have impressed themselves
with double force upon my mind. To the last—the
very last of these—I am already hastening, for my self-
imposed task will soon be over, and the end is near
at hand. In the meanwhile, however, and before the
final hour shall strike, it behoves me to make known
to the reader a somewhat suggestive episode, which
occurred in a portion of the country to which the
reader has not yet been introduced. Only so far as
the spot where poor Hunter was murdered has he

s 2

as yet followed me, but now I must request him to proceed still further along the (for some few miles) frightful moorland waste, till such time as, advancing nearer to the mountains, a rich prospect of wild heather-clad scenery gradually unfolds itself.

But previous to entering the narrow gorge—mysterious of aspect—with its cloud-capped heights, and giant shoulders over-lapping sinuous valleys, there is a village, one whose moral aspect jars painfully—as the traveller wends his slow way along—upon his thoughtful mind. To whom, maybe he asks, belongs that moorland tract, desolate almost beyond belief? Whose are the cabins, from beneath the black and rotting thatch of which rush tribes of almost naked savages, clamouring—as though with one voice, but with fifty outstretched filthy hands—for " charity " from the passers by ?

"Giv' me a ha'penny for the honour o' God." "Only one ha'penny," &c., and as the car slowly, for there is a steep hill to climb, advances towards the shibeen house, where the horse will enjoy a " sup o' male and wather," the semi-naked creatures, keeping with apparent difficulty upon their persons their scant and wretched rags, hold on behind, or to the shafts, their fleshless limbs and pale, thin faces

sufficiently attesting the fact that hunger and they—
poor things !—are old acquaintances.

And this "estate," one which for *apparent*
wretchedness of management, and as a specimen of
the utter demoralisation and abject misery of its
tenantry, deserves to be placed in the foremost rank
of cases such as these, belongs, the enquiring
traveller will be told, to an Englishman!   An
Englishman, and (Heaven save the mark !) a Roman
Catholic, who during the famine bought the property for a comparatively small sum ; and content,
it may be, with getting a certain moderate per-
centage for his money, troubled himself but little
more about his purchase.   Grievous was it to see
those fierce-looking, less than half-clothed young
barbarians, who, shameless, ignorant, and cursed
with the terrible taint of scrofula (at least such was
evidently in many instances the case) defaced by
their presence the fair aspect of Nature, and sent a
thrill of horrified pity through the hearts of those
whom habit had not rendered callous to the spectacle
of human degradation.

On one well-remembered day in earliest autumn,
an old Mayo inhabitant found himself travelling
along the road, which led from the village of Mul-

rany to the beautiful Mountain Pass which bears a
similar appellation. As usual, the throng of beg-
garly cotter tenants pertinaciously followed the
carriage, amongst them being one full-grown girl,
whose long and utterly unclothed limbs, as their
owner ran fleetly by the road side, were—accustomed as the beholder had long been to sights of a
similar description—not a little startling. As is the
case in most Irish villages, a neat and conspicuous
building, known as the quarters of the "Royal Irish
Police," figures in Mulrany, as does also a National
School House. At the entrance to the latter, a
private carriage, drawn by such post horses as the
country affords, was standing as the individual of
whom I write passed that way, and, as chance
would have it, there emerged at that moment from
the doorway no less a personage than the then
Chief Secretary for Ireland, whilst, waiting, as in
duty bound, obsequiously upon his every word and
nod, there could be recognised the Police Serjeant
and the National Schoolmaster.

Having been informed that the Chief Secretary
was making a tour of inspection in the West, the
traveller halted, in his turn, in order to hold converse with the Right Honourable Representative of

the Government. But few were the words which passed between them; those of the traveller being simply expressive of a conviction that *now*, the visiting official having actually *seen* the condition of the poor in the Far West, the rulers of the land would at last have the real truth reported to them. The reply made by the Chief Secretary, although it was word for word repeated to me, has altogether escaped my memory, but, as a proof (if any such indeed were wanting) of the little real interest taken by England in the well-being of the poor in Ireland, I may here mention that neither the poverty-stricken aspect of wretched Mulrany, nor the "humble petition" of my unimportant friend, had any effect on the report eventually drawn up by the "Chief Secretary." It suited the *then* existing Government (as indeed appears to be the case with most Governments) to represent the condition of Ireland as entirely flourishing, and prosperous. There are chronic evils, and the state of the poor in the Far West would appear to be amongst them, which are alike too weighty and too unpleasant to be handled by our Rulers in London. Whether if the Pandora's box containing so much that requires cleansing, were to be thrown wide open,

Hope would be found lying *perdu* at the bottom, is a problem which has yet to be solved.

But I am delaying too long on my. way to the Pass, the beauty of which I have as yet only hinted at. Between high mountains, richly clothed to a considerable elevation, with " Mediterranean " heather, the road winds through the narrow defile. To the height of fully six feet, and with a luxuriance of growth not inferior to that on which the eye of the traveller rests as he journeys along the Maremma Coast road, this charming shrub is seen. In early spring, *pinky-white* blossoms in bright profusion cover its every spray and twig, whilst, as the summer advances, the thickly growing shrubs are one mass of glorious dark green foliage. This beautiful plant is indigenous in the neighbourhood of Mulrany, as well as on the shores of Treenlaur Lake, and for a short distance on the Mayo side of the Killery Bay. Nowhere, however, does it flourish in such rich perfection as at Mulrany. The so-called " Connemara heather " on the contrary, is not to be found in the country anywhere save in the Irish Highlands beyond Westport, but, as I have heard, it is not uncommon in the mountains of Portugal. This plant is capricious, and will not bear transplanting. It is covered with a profusion of bells of a rich crimson colour, and fully two-thirds of an inch in length.

Onward, onward, past the frowning mountains, onward, with, on my left, a shallow inlet of the sea, on which picturesque fishermen are dredging for oysters, whilst before me (but with many an intervening mile across what may often in truth be called a howling wilderness), there rises a beacon tower! Ah! how often, when the fierce Connaught wind has howled around my "outside car," threatening at each moment to upset it, and when the ruthless blasts, sweeping over the moorland waste, have sent a wintry chill throughout my frame, have I been cheered upon my dreary pilgrimage by the sight of that distant tower on the beetling rock—that tower within whose walls sojourned yearly for a brief space those whose well-remembered voices were to my fancy's ear,

"Like far off music voyaging the breeze."

Warm was the welcome that I knew awaited me, and bright as sunshine in a shady place would, I know, be the smile of the one friend I loved and trusted then : but they are gone now, "the old familiar faces," and to my sad heart the memory of that beacon tower on the rock is as "a dream within a dream."

    *   *   *   *   *

Something, but methinks scarcely enough, have I said in these pages of the strength of family affection which exists amongst this portion of the Celtic race. In comparison with either the peasant inhabitants of La Basse Bretagne, (so many of whose customs and habits closely resemble those of the Connaught Celts,) or with the northern Welsh, the Irish according to my experience, decidedly—as regards the warmth of their "near frindships "—bear away the palm. As one proof that it is so, I have only to mention the large sums of money which the emigrants send from distant lands to their loved ones at home, loved ones, in many cases, whom they cannot expect ever to see again in this world, but who, because "out of sight," are very far from "out of mind." *In* England, and *by* the English it is, in my opinion, far too common a custom to speak of the Irish generally in terms of opprobrium and contempt. The vices of lying, treachery, ingratitude, and cheating are universally ascribed to those who have been unlucky enough to obtain that unfortu-

nate possession a " bad name." That such qualities
are, to a certain extent, characteristics of the inhabitants of Roman Catholic Ireland, I do not attempt
to deny, but let those who hastily condemn them
reflect in an impartial spirit upon the " past " of this
people, and some excuse may, perhaps, be found for
them. Centuries of poverty and oppression, during
which only the worst qualities incidental to human
nature were called into requisition; centuries, during
which the struggle to *live* entailed not only the commission of " dirty deeds," but the deterioration both
of individual and national character which therefrom
naturally ensues ; such are among the causes which
have earned for the Celts the character under which
they groan. But there are, besides, still stronger
excuses to be urged for them ; and when, amongst
these, I name the religious despotism beneath
which the people have for generations trembled,
methinks that no dispassionate observer will deny
to the Roman Catholic Irish the benefit of " extenu-
ating circumstances." Of the " Faith " which has
so greatly tended to make them what they are,
these poor blind followers of an interested priesthood
have no opportunity of either seeing or hearing the
lovely, the softening, and the ennobling side. By no

sound of swelling organ, or of voices raised in mingling strains of beauty towards the throne of Heaven, are their senses roused to higher aspirations, or to a tenderer love towards the creatures to whom the same God that bade the power of music be, has given the breath of life. Only on the debasing side of human nature can their mental vision dwell, and only on the lowest of the passions, *Fear*, do their remorseless tyrants work. That "honour" should be to them a thing utterly unknown, and "keeping faith" with their neighbours an unacknowledged duty, is far from surprising when we reflect that in their priests' own published catechism (the one to which I have before alluded) these words are found, "A promise need not be kept, if, after making it, circumstances arise which make it inconvenient to fulfil its provisions." The hope held out in the Bible of a blessing upon the man who "sweareth to his neighbour and disappointeth him not, though it were to his own hindrance," differs in this, as in many other instances, so entirely from priestly teaching, that the keeping of the Holy Scriptures as sealed books from their flocks seems the "most natural thing in life."

To expect a people, whose moral deterioration has been the work of ages, to lose in a "twinkling" their acquired characteristics is simply absurd. Grieved was I, yet not surprised, that those who had been ready, in the days of my *power* to aid them, to fawn upon and to flatter, should, when only the *will* to serve remained, have met me with cold ingratitude, ay, even with contumely and insult. Not in a day, nor in a century, can better things, as regards Celtic nature, be hoped for. In due course of time, and under the circumstances of a banished clerical tyranny, and a resident and kindly aristocracy, some amelioration might be looked for; but, as has been so often and so ineffectually asked, how are these blessings to be attained? The Celtic race in Ireland are, so says public opinion, distinguished as being troublesome, ungrateful, false; but, even though the accusation be a true one, should they not meet with the allowances for their national faults which other peoples have, and not in vain, laid claim to?

In very many respects the Irish character assimilates with the Gallic—excitable, unstable, and—to a great extent, and partly because of the Gasconading propensities of each—untrustworthy. Can we wonder that the Irish, under circumstances so widely different from the French, should have degenerated into what they (the Celts)—in too many instances—are?

Before closing this chapter, it is, I think, expedient, seeing that the vexed questions affecting the respective rights of landlords and their poorer class of tenants is now, in a more than usual degree, occupying public attention, to say a few more words on this important subject.

As far as my experience can be trusted, the fact is undoubted, that on 50,000 acres or so of mountain and moorland, let, previous to the Irish famine, to "small" tenants, the poor cotters, who clung like "grim death" to their miserable holdings, *could not* pay the rent and also live and clothe themselves. Thirty per cent. higher than that of our yearly rental was that which the peasant tenantry collectively paid (or were supposed to do so) into the landlord's exchequer. In a climate where rain is the rule, and a fine day the exception, it is *only* as grazing land, and that on an extensive scale, that a "living" can—on such a soil—be made. Truly an object of pity is the wretched peasant whose cut but "unsaved" turf lies, week after week and month after month, rotting on the ground; whose "little lock of oats," destitute of sun wherewith to ripen it, is to him a dead loss as it "grows,"—melancholy spectacle,—in the sheaf; whilst almost equally precarious is the crop of *praties*, on which his brightest hopes are built, cursed as he is with a "long wake family." For the "rint," as certainly as the dreaded day of reckoning comes round, *must*, on pain of eviction, be promptly paid, and then, God help him, if the lord of the soil does not, after the generous fashion so lately set by the Earl of Westmeath, in County Galway, have mercy on the defaulter, and (inasmuch as "he has not wherewith to pay") forgive him a portion of his debt.

Harsh as the word "eviction" sounds, it is often nevertheless on the landlord's part the truest mercy towards the poverty-stricken ones, to force them to find a home elsewhere. To this conviction I adhere, and I defy any one really conversant with the subject to prove that the existence of such a class of tenants as I have endeavoured to describe can tend to the advantage of any,—save, possibly, the "clairgy," who exist upon the dues extorted from the superstitious terrors of the poor.

CHAPTER XXVII.

DESERTION OF THE COAST BY FISH.—MICKY SHANAHAN, THE SPY.—"POOR SCHOLARS" PECULIAR TO IRELAND.

AMONGST other concomitant evils with which this ill-fated country was visited in the famine years, that of the almost entire desertion of the coast by the shoals of fish, which had once been a boon beyond price to the people, was not the least remarkable. The "herring fishery," as a source of wealth, was, after the year 1847, as a thing of the past; nor did that inferior fish, the mackerel, make up by his presence—his presence, that is to say, in thousands at a time—for other defalcations. Once, and once only, did we see a big haul of these fish drawn to land. Four thousand mackerel, if I recollect rightly, were then and there captured; but as a rule the *Seine* net was (even when the mackerel in shoals were known to be "in," and when the rush of rippling water gave sure tokens of their presence), to the blank despair of the toilers of the sea, drawn in as empty of finny prey as when, with wild excitement both of voice and gesture, the net was flung into the tranquil waters.

Whales are not rare visitors on the western coast, but it is only in still weather, and when the summer sun shines brightly, that they, in rolling, tumbling numbers, venture into the Killery Bay. As a matter of course, the hand of every man is against them, as with miniature water spouts playing from their broad black heads the awkward creatures, after their peculiar fashion,

"Dance and play and wrinkled care beguile."

On come, in their heavy boats, the more than half wild Galway "boys," ready to dispute with all comers their right to the fish.   Out are thrown their herring nets; and shouts, such as only Connaught throats can utter, break, mingled with the sound of clumsy oars, upon the slumbering air; but in a moment of time fell disappointment takes the place of eager hope. Torn to shreds is the strong snare with which the silly fellows had thought to encompass their prey; and had we not presented to them, by way of consolation, a huge monster which our sailors had succeeded in harpooning, terribly crestfallen would have felt the luckless crew as they went slowly back, each man to his humble home amongst

the mountains. The whale was sold to a fish-dealer
at Leenane, for our men, although I informed them
that in an island near America " whale beef " was a
staple article of food, altogether declined to "set
a tooth " in the unwieldy animal we had captured.

" It has a wild taste, the crathur," said the spokes-
man of the party, whom hunger or curiosity had
once tempted to make trial of the untempting-look-
ing "flesh" of a harmless "bottle nose."

What I noticed in the Far West of harsh usage
towards living fishes inclined me to " hope against
hope " that what educated brothers of the "gentle
art " say is true, and that their victims, being " cold-
blooded," do not *feel*. The rough Galway and Mayo
fishermen would seem, however, to hold—judging
from the following fact—a different creed.

The entire coast, and especially the Killery waters,
swarm with huge dog-fish, *alias* sharks. Terribly
rapacious are they; " one " (to invert the sense,
if any exists in Wordsworth's well known line)
" feeding like forty " on the salmon and white trout,
tearing the nets to pieces, and rendering themselves
generally obnoxious to all who suffer from their
depredations. Unpleasant animals they doubtless
are ; but it will, I think, be hardly believed that,

previous to the Saxon rule, when the act of cruelty was strictly forbidden, the Bundoragha fishermen were in the habit of wreaking their vengeance on their hated enemies in the following manner :—

When one of the monsters was, by ill luck to himself, taken in the toils, a stick, sharpened at each end to a point, was made ready, and then incontinently thrust through both the wretched creature's eyes. He would in this guise be then thrown back into the waste of waters, there to " dree his doom."

Now whether the dog-fish did or did not suffer agony from this treatment, certain it is that his tormentors—keen observers for the most part—believed that such a result would follow. If they did not so believe, with what object was a deed so apparently barbarous done ? Not, surely, "*pour décourager les autres*," or to scare away by such a strange abnormal sight young *puppy* fish who might be following in their fathers' footsteps. No ; the Irish are good haters, and revenge is very sweet to them, and therefore it is that, hoping and trusting (even as does a cruel moral torturer, when *only* on the sensitive and tender-hearted he inflicts his wounds) that agony long and terrible will be suffered by the blinded victim, the Celtic fisherman, thirsting for vengeance, rejoices over the hated sufferer as it slowly glides away.

How calm and still on a fine July day are the tranquil waters! All nature for the time seems asleep. The tide is low, and on the jagged rocks the yellow seaweed meets—kissing its own bright likeness—which line for line is repeated clearly upon the unruffled surface of the Bay, as though photographed by an artist's hand. White gulls, dazzling as unstained snow, in countless numbers are flying, screaming, and, for one brief moment, settling upon the water, for the "white-bait" (infant herrings) have "come in," and have, for the nonce, (so prodigious are the shoals thereof,) made *thick* the wide, deep waters of the Killery inlet. With a fine landing-net they are hauled up by millions, whilst the seaweed glitters as though with molten silver, by reason of the hundreds that escape, to die, poor things, an *unfried* death upon the strand.

When I speak of the fish as having deserted the Western Coast, I do not mean to imply that we, individually, suffered from the loss which such a wholesale exodus would imply. With trouble, and labour, by setting spillets, and, when needful, by venturing a good way out to sea, we could always reckon on a "dish" for dinner. Whiting were often plentiful, as were whiting poults, an excellent fish. Fluke, too, that is, small flounders, were common enough sometimes, whilst occasionally a John Dory, and more frequently a skate, would take our bait. Then there was trawling in the open sea, when a few turbot and small soles would by good luck be taken. Lobsters became less plentiful year by year, and oysters, by reason not only of poachers, but of strong winds and tides, did not increase as they were in duty bound to do. In short, let unbelievers on the subject say what they will, and lay all the blame of "neglecting so valuable an article of human food" upon the idleness and unthrift of the people, I maintain that fish—as an article for the attainment of which time and capital may with prudence be risked—does not exist upon the Irish Coast, for the reason that the supply is scanty,

It is the tenth month of the swiftly passing year. October with its equinoctial gales, its chilling rains, and quickly shortening days, has nearly run its length, and already the summit of the mountain which overhangs the house is white with snow. The "world's comforter" sets, for us, very early now. Scarcely do we know the moment when his "hot task" is ended in the West, and seeing that such a proceeding affects no one's comfort or convenience save our own, our clocks are, according to custom at this season of the year, set an hour earlier than the "time of day." By this simple means we *seem* to gain an hour of daylight. Before the sun has fairly risen, we are afoot, and at night "gentle sleep" is wooed by us at an hour (say *nine*, for more than one of the small household), which, by those who live in towns, and take their pleasure late, would of a surety be deemed "unearthly."

Already, hungering after their wonted crumbs, my pretty pensioners, the robins, follow me about the garden paths for food. The pugnacious little darlings abound in our "demesne," and their welcome, together with that of the one Scotch terrier which during a two months' absence I leave behind me, has ever been warm enough to brighten for one brief moment the over-shadowing mountains with a ray of hopeful sunshine. With the exception of the corn-crake, in the sound of whose monotonous melancholy cry I sympathised, the increase, after our advent, of "common" birds in our immediate neighbourhood was year after year very remarkable. Thrushes, blackbirds, yellow hammers, wrens (an object of superstitious hatred to the Irish), and especially cuckoos, were in "wild profusion" in our midst. The last named were often so near and so noisy as to be almost nuisances, one bird answering another after the fashion of domestic cocks; but where they lived and roosted, and why they should, for their *habitat,* choose the bleak, wet moorlands, where for the "soles of their feet" there seemed so little rest, I never could, and probably never shall, understand.

But to return to the autumn time, when the robins are fighting, pecking, fluttering with puffed out feathers, two upon each of my shoulders, whilst a combat *à l'outrance,* for the sake of the good things I am about to scatter on the path, is working up to fever pitch the fury of the red-waistcoated duellists. Suddenly, at one entrance to the garden gate I hear a noise, also one of furious import, but inasmuch as the twitter of angry birds is but a trifle compared to the outbreaks of human anger, so was the sense of fear (one which in truth had latterly rarely slept within me) stirred by the sounds I heard. They proceeded (the unpleasant ones at least, and they were very shocking) from the lips of a man only half-covered with rags, who, standing near the house door, was literally foaming at the mouth with passion. The fellow, Micky O'Shane by name, had

for years been known to us as a rather troublesome
specimen of a class that is peculiar to this country,
and which therefore is, I am half inclined to think,
a consequence of the exclusive use, during many
generations, of that useful but impoverishing esculent
—the potatoe. A creature, half-idiot, but cunning
to a frightful extent withal, was Micky O'Shane, one
who might, had he been given the "larning," have
figured as a "poor scholar," and have repeated—as I
have known such singular, half-witted individuals to
do—a thousand lines of Virgil (in the original) at a
stretch. But Micky, instead of having the "larning,"
was ignorant as a savage; as a savage, too, he was un-
couth, and violent and revengeful, and in consequence
of these agreeable qualities, the country people,
fearing him as an enemy (and withal being under
the impression that if a "traveller," when refused a
night's lodging, died upon the road, those who would
not take him in were legally answerable for his death),
never either sent Micky away empty-handed, or
refused him a "sup o' male" and the shelter, such
as it was, which their miserable cabins afforded.
The man's powers of walking were almost super-
human. Here and there and everywhere in "the
two counties," would he be; and "sorra a ha'porth

did any man know how the crathur slipped along." He was amusing for a short while after his fashion, but scarcely safe to encourage in much "talk," the balance of his mind being very frail, and the upsetting of it an easy thing. A poor half starved, and (excepting when stirred up to wrath by his fanatical hatred against the "joompers") a harmless half idiot was, in our opinion, the ugly, ungainly creature who, whenever he came our way, was certain to receive, from motives of compassion for the lonely wayfarer, not only the meal to which, with the accustomed words, "I'm expecting me dinner," he laid claim, but some cast-off garment, a pair of knickerbockers, it might be, or a well worn shooting-coat, wherewith we sent him on his way rejoicing. But there came a time (it was during the worst Fenian panic) when whispers reached us that Micky was a dangerous character. It was a season when secret rebellion of more kinds than one lurked in the air, and when our enemies the priests were diligently, but in secret, working mischief to the Saxon and to Saxon rule. The sin of which Micky was accused (and rightfully, as full soon appeared) was that of being the "clergy's" *spy*. A long-eared, crafty rascal, his simplicity was more than half assumed, whilst his great

powers of memory and extreme fleetness of foot well
fitted him for an office which rendered it prudent
to avoid as much as possible the use of pen and ink.
As soon as his real character became thoroughly
apparent, Micky's perquisites at the Lodge were,
very naturally, put a stop to. No more trousers
and "sorra a rag" of a blanket was there for one who
was found guilty of pursuing a trade so ignoble and
so treacherous. With well-deserved vituperation,
and with, besides, a strength of language which
he had never heard before from "the masther's"
lips, Micky was duly warned that, if ever he again
set foot upon the Dhulough lands, sundry pains
and penalties awful to think of would be his portion.
For a minute or so the creature remained silent,
but the expression—all animal—of his repulsive face
grew every moment more horrible, and at length
such a storm of execrations, such a fierce howl of
maledictions burst from the wretch's lips, that all
involuntarily I stopped my ears in terror and affright;
for it was on our heads, the heads of the "eternally
damned Protestants" (as in his mad rage he called
us) that Micky showered his anathemas. Truly,
if only a hundredth part of the bad things he hoped
would befall his former benefactors should in very

deed be meted out to them, their worst enemies
might be inclined to think that they had had enough
in the way of punishment to last them for a life.

Long after "mad" Micky had taken himself away,
the memory of his hideous yells remained with me,
and in a weariness and dejection of which I felt
ashamed (for do not curses, as the old proverb says,
always return upon the head of him who utters
them?)—I took refuge from a driving storm of rain
within the walls which had for well nigh a quarter of
a century bidden defiance to the gales which shook (or
seemed to do so), the edifice to its foundation. The
crazy King's exordium to the winds in *his* day might,
I think, have been obeyed in ours, for never since, in
any quarter of the world, have I heard the wild blast
make the heavens echo, as it did at Dhulough, with
the prolonged cadence of its revelry. On the in-
hospitable coast where—according to Froude—the
Flag-ship of the Spanish admiral was, in the year
of grace 1588, wrecked, the "cheeks" of a full-
blown Atlantic gale must certainly, to the gorgeous
grandees who roamed along wet Black Sod Bay, have
appeared to run no slight risk of being—by dint of
over exertion—"cracked!"

CHAPTER XXVIII.

It was my last summer in the West. Never again, on my return from a short sojourn in sunnier climes, would I be met at the entrance of sunless Glenumra valley by the weird welcome of pitiless blasts and driving rains with which habit had made me so painfully familiar. Never again—a truth hidden from me then—would I experience the soul-depressing feeling that I was returning to the midst of those who, strive as I would to benefit them, and to do my duty by them, bore me no love, and had—beyond the empty words "yer honour's welcome home"—no pleasant looks and kindly greeting for my ears.

Strangely enough, the Gaelic name for the "lower regions" is *ifrin*, a word derived from *i-bhuirn* which, being interpreted, means the "Island of incessant rain," and truly there have been times when

on re-entering, after a brief absence, that chill and
solitary defile, the sad swell of the mountain winds has
sounded like "the dirge of murdered hope;" but on
this occasion, whether it was that the secret influence
of the "last time" lay heavily upon my spirits, or
that weightier sorrows, and far keener anxieties
than merely personal grievances, threw the latter
into the shade, must remain an unanswered question;
certain however, is it that on this my last return to
the scenes, which in these pages I have attempted to
describe, I was vaguely, and with something of a not
unpleasing melancholy, conscious of the apathy—the
numbness, if it may be so described, of heart and
feeling, which, when life's longest day of summer is
past, creeps over the tired soul and gives it—Rest.

"Heaven from all creatures hides the book of Fate."

But for this merciful arrangement, how terrible
to "brains unencompassed with nerves of steel,"
would be the constant looking for of judgment to
come! But although the pages of the book be not
fully opened, who can deny that many a time and
often a still small voice whispers to the watchful
ones a warning of the terrible "to come"? And
yet—and yet—prepared as we may think ourselves,

the dreaded hour (as a thief in the night), makes
its approach at last, and finds us—*sleeping !*

> "Who telleth a tale of unspeaking death ?
>   Who lifteth the veil of what is to come ?
> Who painteth the shadows that are beneath
>   The wide winding eaves of the peopled tomb ?
> Or uniteth the hope of what shall be
> With the fears and the love of that which we see ? "

*　　*　　*　　*　　*

Very terrible was the " dead calm " which, when
the brave ruling spirit had departed, crept over
the household. I wandered along the rain-soaked
paths, those paths which I had so often trodden in
restlessness of foot, and with a heart yearning—oh !
so eagerly—to find myself once more amongst the
social and the sympathising of my kind, and now that
yearning seemed to have passed away for ever. I had
deeply sorrowed—and not the less so, in that to none
save to my inner self was the bitterness of my heart
betrayed—over the many wasted years which had
dragged—amongst a strange people—in friendless-
ness and far from kith and kin— their slow length
along. And now those years were over—the tie that
had so long held me bound had snapped asunder—
and I was Free ! Free ! but oh, how sadly ! The

world was "all before me where to choose my place of rest!" But—so strange a thing is human nature, or rather, so strangely works upon us feeble mortals the sickness which is born of hope deferred, that, when freedom came, all hunger after "change" had—as the "baseless fabric" of a dream—vanished into nothingness! Like the aged prisoner, who, grown friendly with his chains, regained his freedom with a sigh, I clung to the quiet to which I had, after long years, become habituated ; and grieved with a bitterness of spirit, which only the desolate can understand, or sympathise with, for the home which was to be mine no longer.

It is autumn time once more, and the writer of these pages, who had so long felt as a grievance the shutting out daily from her view of one of Nature's grandest spectacles, is gazing from a pebbly sea-beach, upon a sunset, lovely and bright as those, which—contemplated from the same spot—Chateaubriand has—in his sweet, flowing verse—immortalised. Swathed in imperial purple, and crowned with molten gold, reposing in bold relief against a background of palest primrose, the "red god" sinks beneath the watery horizon to rest.

Watching the line of light, which gradually towards the "burning west" is slowly gliding, the friendless pilgrim upon life's highway shivers beneath the fresh sea-breeze of late October; but, till the last thread-like filament of sunlight has disappeared behind the distant waves, she lingers—a dreaming, desolate one—upon the deserted shore.

At last the curtain—grey and sombre—falls; her dog (did she say that she was friendless?) barks his request for home and supper, and he has—inasmuch as for her there now exists naught else that she can indulge and yield obedience to—his accustomed way.

> "Gone are the last faint flashes,
>   Set is the sun of her years;
> And over a few poor ashes
>   She sits in her darkness and tears."

THE END.

BRADBURY, AGNEW, & CO., PRINTERS, WHITEFRIARS.